I0438725

Triggered Surface Slips in Southern California Associated with the 2010 El Mayor-Cucapah, Baja California, Mexico, Earthquake

By Michael J. Rymer, Jerome A. Treiman, Katherine J. Kendrick, James J. Lienkaemper, Ray J. Weldon, Roger Bilham, Meng Wei, Eric J. Fielding, Janis L. Hernandez, Brian P. E. Olson, Pamela J. Irvine, Nichole Knepprath, Robert R. Sickler, Xiaopeng Tong, and Martin E. Siem

Prepared in cooperation with the California Geological Survey; University of Oregon; University of Colorado; University of California, San Diego; and Jet Propulsion Laboratory, California Institute of Technology.

Open-File Report 2010–1333

Jointly published as California Geological Survey Special Report 221

U.S. Department of Interior
U.S. Geological Survey

U.S. Department of the Interior
KEN SALAZAR, Secretary

U.S. Geological Survey
Marcia K. McNutt, Director

U.S. Geological Survey, Reston, Virginia: 2011

This report and any updates to it are available online at:
http://pubs.usgs.gov/of/2010/1333/

For more information on the USGS—the Federal source for science about the Earth,
its natural and living resources, natural hazards, and the environment—visit
http://www.usgs.gov or call 1-888-ASK-USGS

For an overview of USGS information products, including maps, imagery, and publications,
visit http://www.usgs.gov/pubprod

Suggested citation:
Rymer, M.J., Treiman, J.A., Kendrick, K.J., Lienkaemper, J.J., Weldon, R.J., Bilham, R., Wei, M., Fielding, E.J.,
Hernandez, J.L., Olson, B.P.E., Irvine, P.J., Knepprath, N., Sickler, R.R., Tong, .X., and Siem, M.E., 2011, Triggered
surface slips in southern California associated with the 2010 El Mayor-Cucapah, Baja California, Mexico, earthquake:
U.S. Geological Survey Open-File Report 2010-1333 and California Geological Survey Special Report 221, 62 p.,
available at http://pubs.usgs.gov/of/ 2010/1333/.

Contents

Figures

Tables

Triggered Surface Slips in Southern California Associated with the 2010 El Mayor-Cucapah, Baja California, Mexico, Earthquake

By Michael J. Rymer[1], Jerome A. Treiman[2], Katherine J. Kendrick[3], James J. Lienkaemper[1], Ray J. Weldon[4], Roger Bilham[5], Meng Wei[6], Eric J. Fielding[7], Janis L. Hernandez[2], Brian P. E. Olson[2], Pamela J. Irvine[2], Nichole Knepprath[1], Robert R. Sickler[1], Xiaopeng Tong[6], and Martin E. Siem[8]

Abstract

The April 4, 2010 (M_w7.2), El Mayor-Cucapah, Baja California, Mexico, earthquake is the strongest earthquake to shake the Salton Trough area since the 1992 (M_w7.3) Landers earthquake. Similar to the Landers event, ground-surface fracturing occurred on multiple faults in the trough. However, the 2010 event triggered surface slip on more faults in the central Salton Trough than previous earthquakes, including multiple faults in the Yuha Desert area, the southwestern section of the Salton Trough. In the central Salton Trough, surface fracturing occurred along the southern San Andreas, Coyote Creek, Superstition Hills, Wienert, Kalin, and Imperial Faults and along the Brawley Fault Zone, all of which are known to have slipped in historical time, either in primary (tectonic) slip and/or in triggered slip. Surface slip in association with the El Mayor-Cucapah earthquake is at least the eighth time in the past 42 years that a local or regional earthquake has triggered slip along faults in the central Salton Trough. In the southwestern part of the Salton Trough, surface fractures (triggered slip) occurred in a broad area of the Yuha Desert. This is the first time that triggered slip has been observed in the southwestern Salton Trough.

Triggered slip in the Yuha Desert area occurred along more than two dozen faults, only some of which were recognized before the April 4, 2010, El Mayor-Cucapah earthquake. From east to northwest, slip occurred in seven general areas: (1) in the Northern Centinela Fault Zone (newly named), (2) along unnamed faults south of Pinto Wash, (3) along the Yuha Fault (newly named), (4) along both east and west branches of the Laguna Salada Fault, (5) along the Yuha Well Fault Zone (newly revised name) and related faults between it and the Yuha Fault, (6) along the Ocotillo Fault (newly named) and related faults to the north and south, and (7) along the southeasternmost section of the Elsinore Fault. Faults that slipped in the Yuha Desert area include northwest-trending right-lateral faults, northeast-trending left-lateral faults, and north-south faults, some of which had dominantly vertical offset. Triggered slip along the Ocotillo and Elsinore Faults appears to have occurred only in association with the June 14, 2010 (M_w5.7), aftershock. This aftershock also resulted in slip along other faults near the town of Ocotillo. Triggered offset on faults in the Yuha Desert area was mostly less than 20 mm, with three significant exceptions, including slip of about 50–60 mm on the Yuha Fault, 40 mm on a fault south of Pinto Wash, and about 85 mm on the Ocotillo Fault. All triggered slips in the Yuha Desert area occurred along preexisting faults, whether previously recognized or not.

[1]U.S. Geological Survey, Menlo Park, Calif.

[2]California Geological Survey, Los Angeles, Calif.

[3]U.S. Geological Survey, Pasadena, Calif.

[4]Department of Geological Sciences, University of Oregon, Eugene, Oregon

[5]CIRES, Department of Geological Sciences, University of Colorado, Boulder, Colo.

[6]Institute of Geophysics and Planetary Physics, Scripps Institution of Oceanography, University of California, San Diego, La Jolla, Calif.

[7]Jet Propulsion Laboratory/California Institute of Technology, Pasadena, Calif.

[8]Construction Testing & Engineering, Escondido, Calif.

Introduction

The M_w 7.2 El Mayor-Cucapah earthquake of April 4, 2010 (Hauksson and others, 2011), resulted in primary, tectonic rupture on many faults in the epicentral area of northern Baja California (Fletcher and others, 2010). The El Mayor-Cucapah earthquake also triggered ground-surface slip on faults in the Salton Trough, to distances of 60–172 km from the epicenter (fig. 1, table 1). The El Mayor-Cucapah earthquake is only the most recent of many local or regional earthquakes within the past four decades to have triggered slip on faults in the Salton Trough. This report documents that the earthquake caused slip on more faults and in a much broader area than reported for previous earthquakes. Our interpretation is that all of the surface slip that is documented in this report represents triggered slip, rather than primary fault rupture. Our interpretations are based on both the distance from the epicenter, as well as the evidence supporting the shallow nature of the slip (Oskin and others, 2011). In this report we use the terms surface slip, surface fracturing, and surface breakage interchangeably to describe the effects of this triggered slip. All of the locations documented herein display lateral displacement, vertical displacement, or a combination of both.

Triggered surface breaks were documented in the Salton Trough following the 1968 Borrego Mountain earthquake (Allen and others, 1972), the 1979 Imperial Valley earthquake (Fuis, 1982; Sieh, 1982), the 1981 Westmorland earthquake (Sharp and others, 1986a), the 1986 North Palm Springs earthquake (Sharp and others, 1986b; Williams and others, 1988), the 1987 Superstition Hills earthquake (Hudnut and Clark, 1989; Sharp, 1989), the 1992 Joshua Tree and Landers earthquakes (Bodin and others, 1994; Rymer, 2000), and the 1999 Hector Mine earthquake (Rymer and others, 2002). Instrumental recordings of triggered slip, aseismic surface slip (creep), and afterslip also were reported for previous events in the Salton Trough (Goulty and others, 1978; Cohn and others, 1982; Louie and others, 1985; McGill and others, 1989, Bilham, 1989; Lyons and others, 2002; Rymer and others, 2002; Wei and others, 2009).

Within the past four decades triggered slip has been documented along the southernmost San Andreas Fault in the southeastern Coachella Valley in five discrete earthquakes (Allen and others, 1972; Sieh, 1982; Williams and others, 1988; Rymer, 2000; Rymer and others, 2002), and in many additional slip pulses as determined by creepmeters and repeated surveys (for example, McGill and others, 1989; Williams and Sieh, 1987; Williams and others, 1988; Rymer and others, 2002), along with episodic dextral creep (Louie and others, 1985; Sieh and Williams, 1990). If such surface movement has occurred throughout the period since the last great earthquake, about 320 years ago (Sieh and Williams, 1990), then the net displacement could add up to tens of centimeters, representing a significant amount of shallow strain release.

This report describes the distribution and amount of triggered slip on the San Andreas, Coyote Creek, Superstition Hills, Wienert, Kalin, and Imperial Faults and the Brawley Fault Zone within the central Salton Trough and multiple faults in the Yuha Desert area of southwestern Salton Trough (fig. 1; table 1). All slips are associated with the 2010 El Mayor-Cucapah earthquake and its aftershocks. Our tectonic interpretations are based on field measurements. In addition, this report briefly presents evidence that faults that moved

in association with the El Mayor-Cucapah earthquake also have subtle late Pleistocene to Holocene scarps, indicating prior displacement. Field evidence documenting the location and amount of slip and the preexistence of fault scarps is presented in the maps, photographs, tables, and appendix. All photographs included in this report are by the first author, unless noted otherwise.

Timing of Fault Slip

Both instrumental recordings and geologic observations constrain triggered slip along faults in the Salton Trough to the time of the El Mayor-Cucapah earthquake. Figure 2 shows creepmeter data from instruments located along the San Andreas and Superstition Hills Faults, indicating that slip occurred as the seismic wave from the El Mayor-Cucapah earthquake passed through the region. Dextral slip was initiated and completed between 5-minute samples bracketing the passage of seismic waves from the El Mayor-Cucapah mainshock on the southernmost San Andreas Fault at Durmid Hill and between 10-minute samples at three other creepmeter sites, two in the central part of Durmid Hill and one on the Superstition Hills Fault (fig. 1; table 2). Also, one of us (M.J.R.) had made field visits to both the Kalin and Imperial Faults within 2 weeks before the El Mayor-Cucapah earthquake, documenting no new slip at that time. These observations, combined with our comprehensive postearthquake searches for surface slip beginning the day after the event, constrain the timing of triggered slip as following the El Mayor-Cucapah earthquake.

Dextral slip recorded by the creepmeters closely correlates with the amount of slip offset measured at the ground surface, with the caveat that creepmeters sample a wider section of the respective faults and are buried about 1 m below the ground surface. This topic was addressed by Rymer (2000), who stated that comparison of triggered slip values along the San Andreas Fault associated with the 1992 Landers earthquake as determined geologically (with about 1-m aperture) to data from creepmeters (Bodin and others, 1994; with aperture about 6–9 m) indicate ~3–7 mm greater dextral slip amounts measured by creepmeters than measured geologically. Comparisons further show that surface breakage does not occur until a threshold of 3–7 mm of recorded creep is reached.

Methods

Slip components were determined by measuring the displacement between matching irregularities in soil blocks or thin soil crusts along the local strike of the affected faults. We measured the slip vector, the azimuth of the slip, and the local strike of the fault; where present, we measured the vertical component of slip and the direction of relative vertical displacement (appendix A).

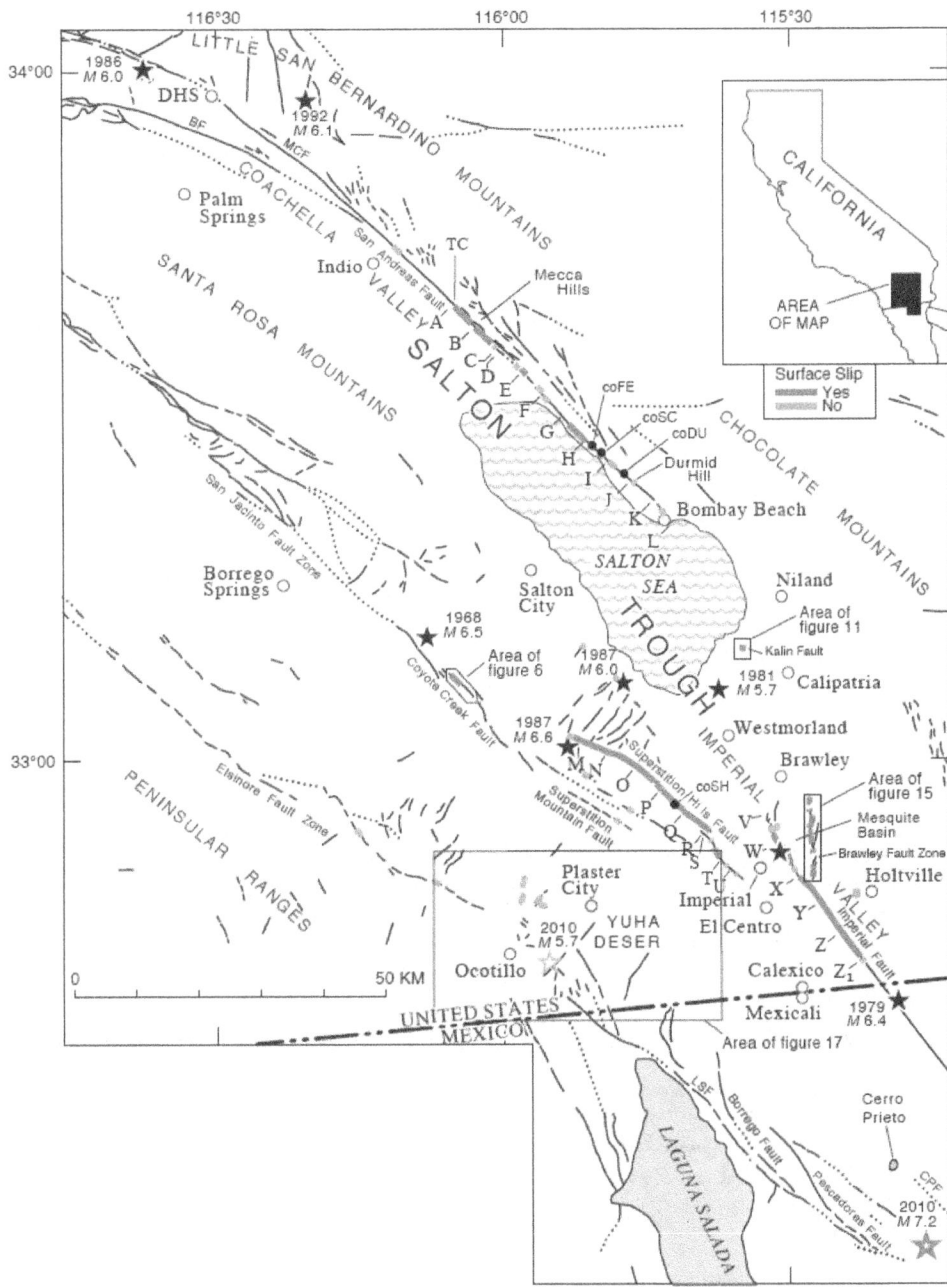

Figure 1. Index map showing Quaternary faults in the greater Salton Trough area (modified from Jennings, 1994). Red bars along faults in central Salton Trough show the generalized location of 2010 surface slip along the San Andreas, Coyote Creek, Superstition Hills, Wienert, Kalin, and Imperial Faults and along the Brawley Fault Zone triggered by the El Mayor-Cucapah earthquake—many additional faults in the Yuha Desert experienced triggered slip (see fig. 17). Green bars along faults show the location of field observations of no slip in 2010. Large red star marks location of El Mayor-Cucapah mainshock epicenter (labeled with magnitude 7.2). Large orange star marks location of June 14, 2010, aftershock (labeled with magnitude 5.7). Small black stars with date and magnitude indicate epicenters of earlier earthquakes that also triggered slip on southern San Andreas, Coyote Creek, Superstition Hills, or Imperial Fault. BF, Banning Fault; DHS, Desert Hot Springs; MCF, Mission Creek Fault; TC, mouth of Thermal Canyon. Letters A to L mark location of ends of strip maps of San Andreas Fault, shown in figure 4; letters M to R mark location of ends of strip maps of Superstition Hills Fault, shown in figure 8; letters S to U mark location of ends of strip maps of Wienert Fault, shown in figure 10; letters V to Z₁ mark location of ends of strip maps of Imperial Fault, shown in figure 13. Black dots show the location of creepmeter stations (coFE, Ferrum; coSC, Salt Creek; coDU, Durmid Hill; and coSH, Superstition Hills).

Table 1. Characteristics of triggered slip along faults in the Salton Trough in 2010.

Fault	Lateral Extent of Triggered Slip along fault[a] (in km)	Distance to Epicenter[b] (in km)	Maximum Slip Value (in mm)
CENTRAL SALTON TROUGH			
San Andreas	29	144–172	18
Coyote Creek	5	119–122	16
Superstition Hills	23	79–99	16
Wienert	0.1[c]	74	5
Kalin	0.01[c]	103	5
Imperial	22	52–73	20
Brawley FZ	13	66–78	20
YUHA DESERT AREA			
Northern Centinela FZ	0.1–3[d]	60–63	10
So. of Pinto Wash	1–3[d]	64–66	40
Yuha	5–7[d]	68–69	49
Laguna Salada, E	6–7[d]	69–74	40
Laguna Salada, W	5–6	71–76	40
Yuha Well FZ	10	76–78	19
Vista de Anza	3–4[d]	76–77	13
Yuha Well	1–4[d]	78	19
Ocotillo FZ	6	6–8[e]	85
Ocotillo	1	6–7[e]	85
Elsinore FZ	0.5	8–9[e]	10

[a] Measured from endpoints of slip; slip along each fault was discontinuous

[b] Measured from epicenter to endpoints of triggered slip from 4 April, 2010 M_w7 2 mainshock or 14 June, 2010 M_w5 7 aftershock

[c] Surface slip may have extended much farther; observations were precluded by dense crops and plowed fields

[d] Range of extent of triggered slip from field-checked (first value) or field- and UAVSAR-interferogram-inferred (second value) observations

[e] Measured from epicenter of M_w5 7 aftershock, which triggered slip on this fault

Table 2. List of operating University of Colorado creepmeters used in this report.

[Data from telemetered instruments may be viewed at https://datagarrison com user geo, password hobo]

Name	Location	Fault[1]	Latitude (deg)	Longitude (deg)	Length (m)	Type	Notes
coFE	Ferrum	SAF	33.45724	-115.85386	9@30	graphite	
coSC	Salt Creek	SAF	33.44850	-115.84370	6@72	stainless	25 mm range
coDU	Durmid Hill	SAF	33.45725	-115.85386	6@30	graphite	no telemetry
coSH	Superstition Hills	SHF	32.93010	-115.70090	6@30	invar	
coBE	Yuha Desert	LSFE	32.6643	-115.8480	6@30	graphite	
coBW	Yuha Desert	LSFW	32.6483	-115.8790	6@30	graphite	

[1] SAF, San Andreas Fault; SHF, Superstition Hills Fault; LSFE, Laguna Salada Fault, east branch; LSFW, Laguna Salada Fault, west branch

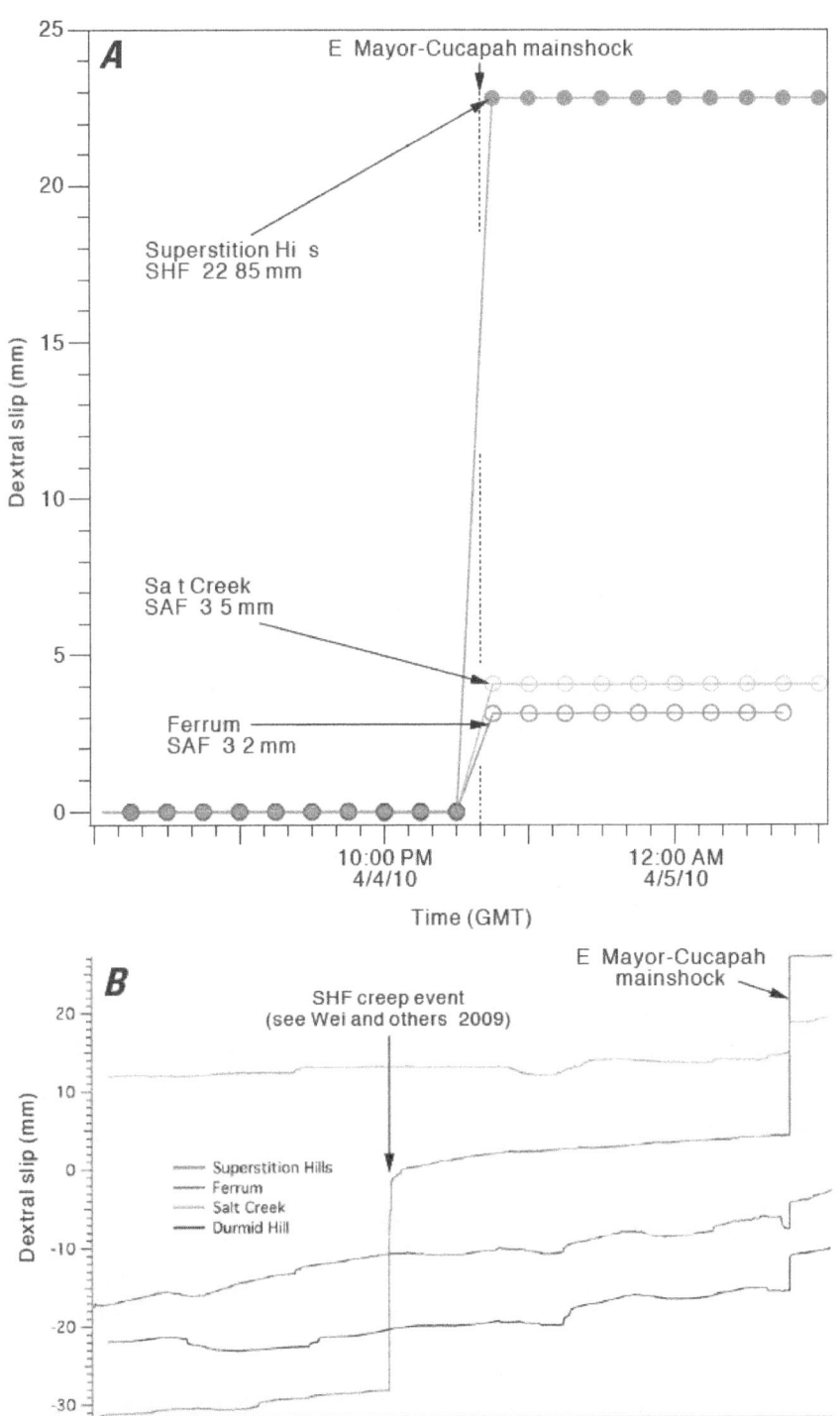

Figure 2. Creepmeter data that show timing of slip on the San Andreas and Superstition Hills Faults in association with the El Mayor-Cucapah earthquake. *A*, Detailed plot of creepmeter data for three sites in a 6-hr period approximately centered on the El Mayor-Cucapah earthquake. Data plotted with normalized zero slip before the earthquake. The circles are 10-minute samples. *B*, Plot of a 6-yr period (2004–2010) of creepmeter data. Included in these data is the start of a large creep event on the Superstition Hills Fault (SHF) in October 2006 (see Wei and others, 2009) compared to the abrupt triggered slip recorded on April 4, 2010. Plot shows low background creep rates on fault segments (1-3 mm/yr) interrupted by episodic creep events and triggered slip. Left-lateral excursions (negative slopes) in the data follow rainfall on Durmid Hill. Note that the creep rates on the San Andreas Fault remain high after the El Mayor-Cucapah earthquake. Transmission problems at both Salt Creek and Ferrum resulted in data gaps following the earthquake that have been interpolated in this plot. The data from Durmid Hill are continuous and confirm the resumption of preseismic creep rates immediately after the triggered slip event. In contrast, the post-earthquake creep rate on the Superstition Hills Fault is slower than the pre-event rate.

Field reconnaissance for surface breakage along faults in the greater Salton Trough began within hours of the April 4, 2010, earthquake and continued episodically until August 7, 2010. Our data provide minimum estimates of the total slip for each fault, given that our observations and measurements span about 0.5 m of fault width. Thus, our data are not directly comparable to data that were collected via other methods, such as InSAR (for example, Wei and others, 2011); our measurements likely underestimate the total slip. In this report, we emphasize the spatial distribution of surface slip and relative amounts of displacement between faults, and thus our data complement other studies by highlighting features that the coarser scale studies miss.

We mapped surface fractures only where they were directly observed and did not extrapolate features through areas of dense agricultural vegetation or loose sand, when encountered, for example, along sections of the Kalin and Imperial Faults, the Brawley Fault Zone, and the Laguna Salada Fault, east branch. We used topographic maps and aerial photographs to focus our searches, along with maps showing the distribution of surface slip in 1968 (Clark, 1972), 1979 (Sharp and others, 1982; Sieh, 1982), and 1987 (Sharp and others, 1989). In the Yuha Desert area we used fault maps of Smith (1979), Clark (1982), Isaac (1986), and Kahle (1988). (See discussion, below, regarding use of UAVSAR interferograms to locate faults that moved, along with the generalized timing of such movements.) We used hand-held GPS receivers to locate field observations.

We determined slip component by measuring the distance between matching piercing points (fig. 3A) and projecting the distance between them onto the measured local strike of the fault. The lateral component of slip was calculated by multiplying the horizontal-slip component by the cosine of the angle between the slip azimuth and the local fault azimuth (fig. 3B). Where present, the vertical component of slip and the direction of relative vertical displacement were also measured. Displacement values were small in the central Salton Trough, nowhere greater than 20 mm; in the Yuha Desert area we measured displacements as large as 85 mm.

San Andreas Fault

Field checks for surface breakage along the San Andreas Fault in the southeastern Coachella Valley began on April 4, the day of the El Mayor-Cucapah earthquake. One of us (R.J.W.) checked the San Andreas Fault in the vicinity of Salt Creek. Two of us (M.W. and X.T.) checked the fault near the mouth of Box Canyon, near North Shore, and between Mecca Beach and Salt Creek on April 7. Two of us (M.J.R. and B.P.E.O.) checked the San Andreas Fault in the areas of Box Canyon, North Shore, Salt Creek, Durmid Hill, and Bombay Beach (figs. 1, 4) on April 8, 2010. Field checks were made in the Indio area and in Mecca Hills (R.J.W.) on April 8 and 9, 2010; additional field checks were made in northwestern part of the Mecca Hills (K.J.K.) on April 14, 2010.

We observed discontinuous surface breaks along the San Andreas Fault over a distance of about 29 km (figs. 1, 4; table 1), spanning distances from the El Mayor-Cucapah epicenter of about 144 and 172 km, from the southeast to the northwest, respectively (table 1). Breaks developed in two broad areas, the Mecca Hills (figs. 5A–C) and between North Shore and Salt Creek (fig. 4, panels A–B, B–C, and G–H). Surface breaks formed predominantly in uplifted Pleistocene fine-grained lacustrine and fluvial deposits.

Discussion

Triggered slip in 2010 along the San Andreas Fault in the southeastern Coachella Valley generally occurred where it had in previous moderate to large earthquakes. The five previous documented slip events, in 1968, 1979, 1986, 1992, and 1999, were triggered by earthquakes of $M5.6–7.3$ whose epicenters were situated at different azimuthal directions (see Rymer and others, 2002, their table 1). Previous slip, in general, occurred along the fault in the Durmid Hill and Mecca Hills areas; two of the earlier events, 1986 and 1992, also triggered slip in the Indio Hills (Williams and others, 1988; Rymer, 2000). See Bilham and Williams (1985) for discussion of structural relations associated with occurrence of triggered slip and Rymer (2000) for review of distribution of triggered slip and local geologic materials.

Figures 5C and D show parts of a large reddish-brown, clay-rich deposit exposed along the San Andreas Fault. Rymer (2000) speculated that this fine-grained, locally stratified (that is, not fault gouge) body likely is tectonically emplaced lacustrine strata. Owing to its fine grain size and thus likelihood to retain water, this body may have aided in development of surface slip. Offset values along the San Andreas Fault were small, mostly between 2 and 5 mm and nowhere greater than 18 mm. Similar to observations of triggered slip in previous events, the largest offset values were measured in the Mecca Hills.

Coyote Creek Fault

Field checks for surface breakage along the Coyote Creek Fault in the northwestern Imperial Valley began 6 days after the El Mayor-Cucapah earthquake. Two of us (J.A.T. and J.L.H.) checked the Coyote Creek Fault on April 10, 2010. Field checks were made in the areas near the Ocotillo Badlands and Old Kane Spring Road (figs. 1, 6).

Discussion

Triggered slip in 2010 along the Coyote Creek Fault in the northwestern Imperial Valley generally occurred exactly where it had in previous moderate to large earthquakes. The two previous documented slip events occurred in 1968 and

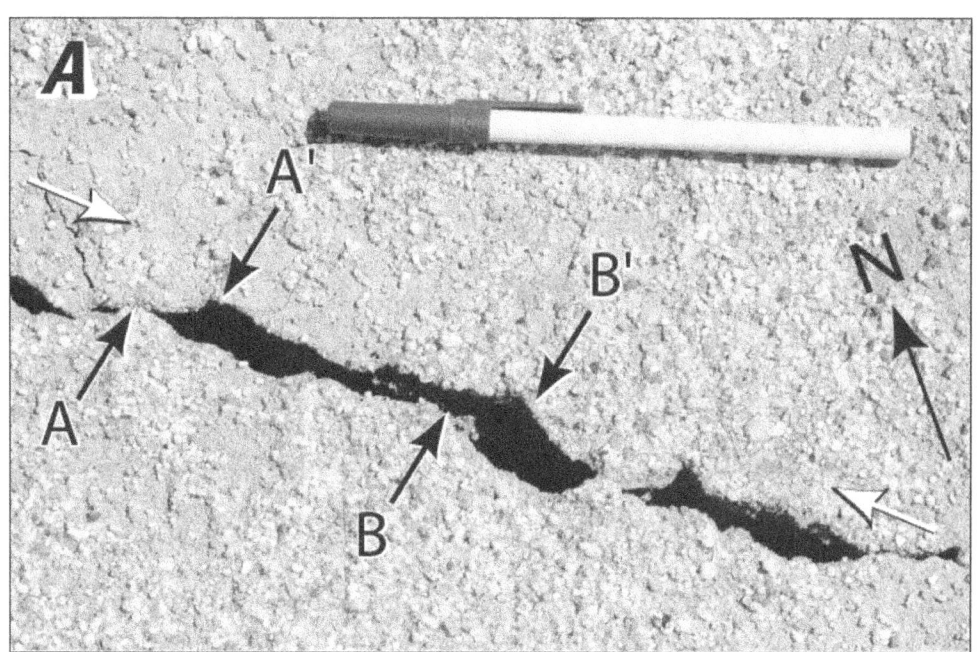

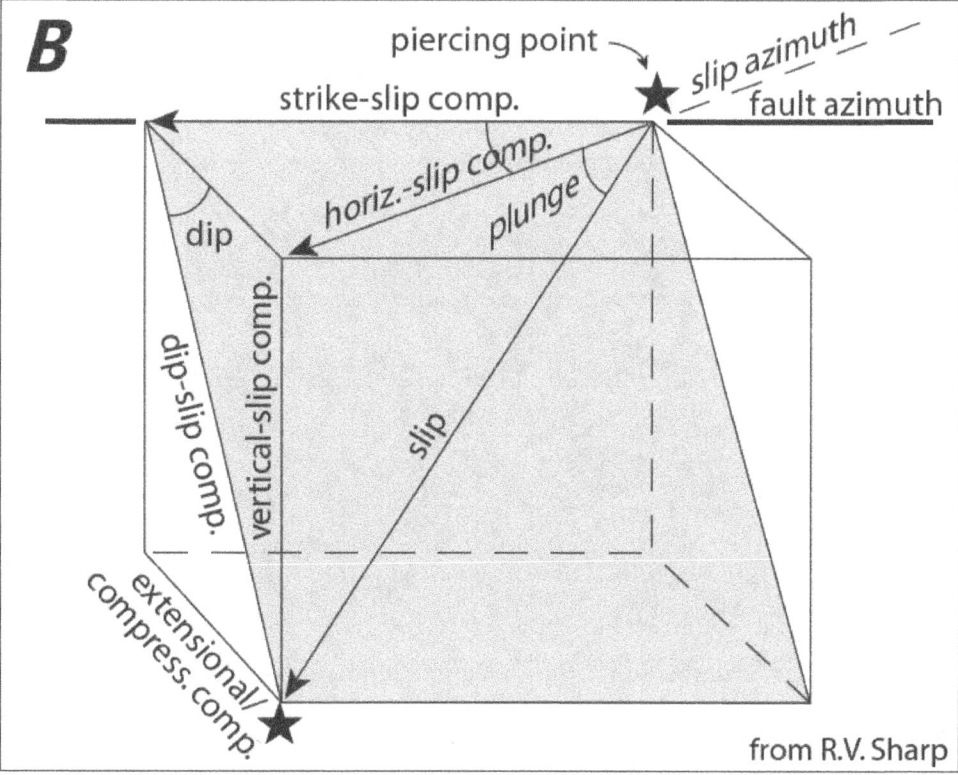

Figure 3. Photograph and diagram showing determination of components of slip. *A,* Photograph of fracture along Laguna Salada Fault, east branch. Corresponding piercing points A and A' and B and B' (black arrows) constrain the calculated amount of right-lateral strike-slip component of displacement (see fig. 25 for location). White arrows, orientation of local fault azimuth. Right-lateral component of displacement at time of photograph was 20 mm; photograph taken April 6, 2010. *B,* Schematic block diagram showing components of fault slip and how to calculate fault parallel component of displacement (see text for explanation).

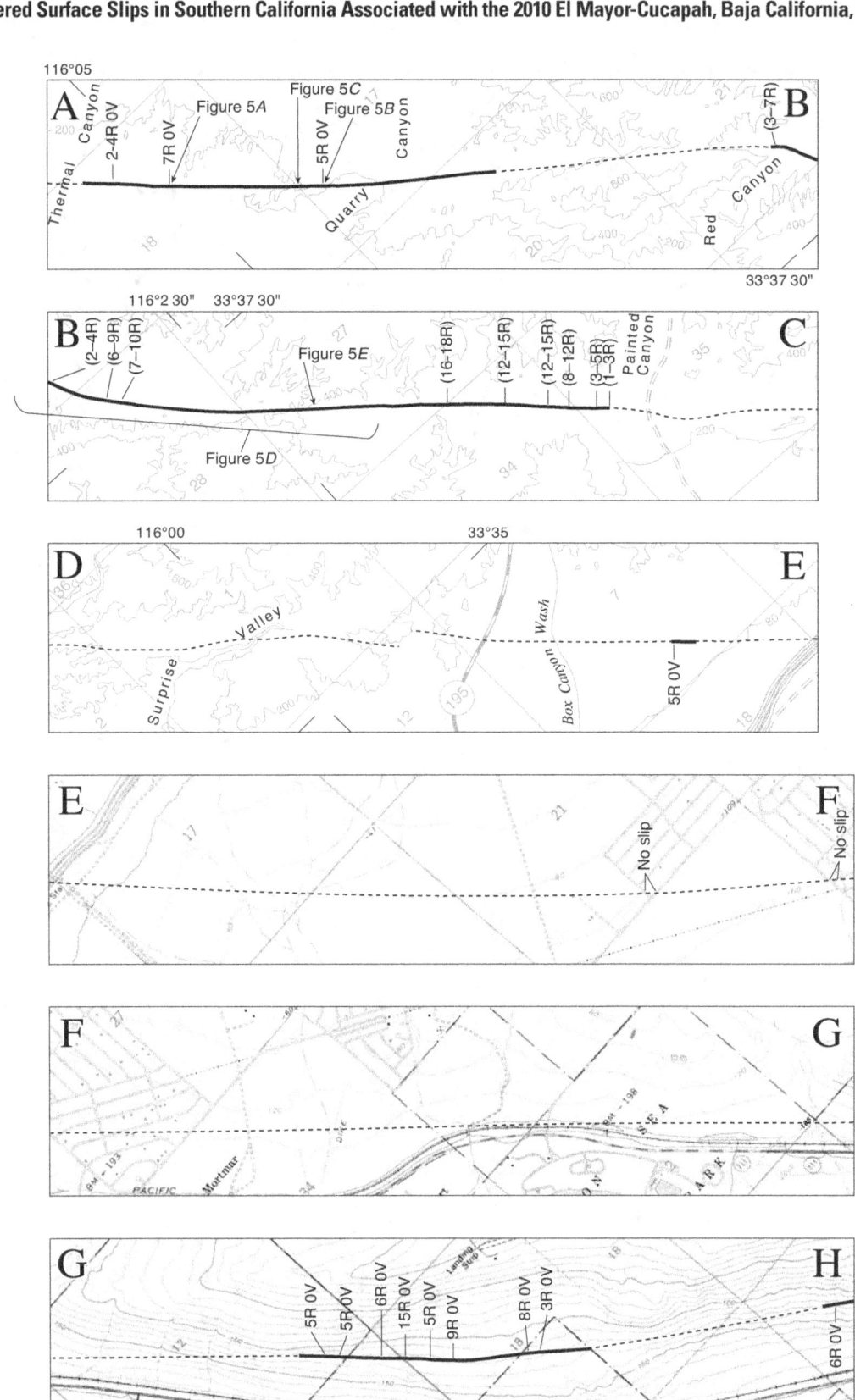

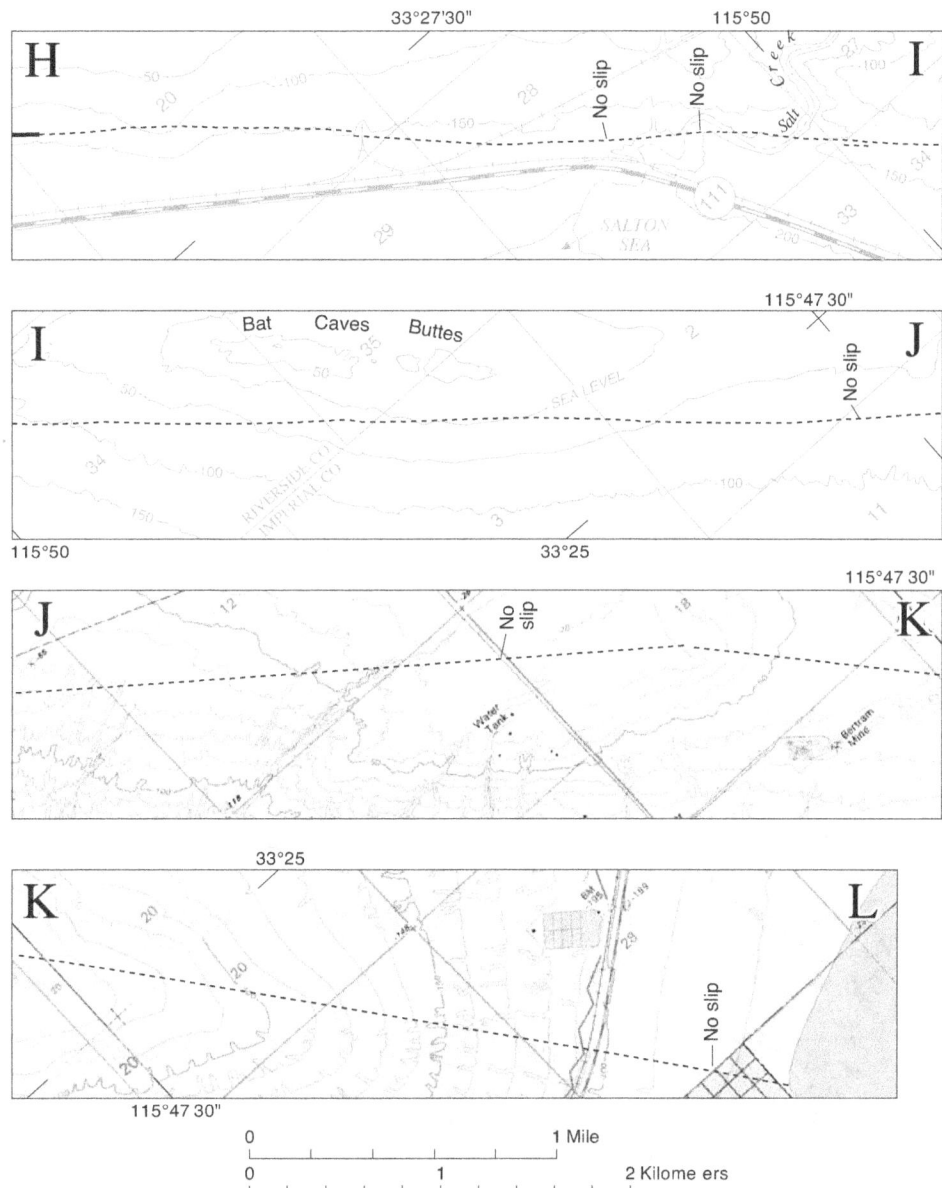

Figure 4. Strip maps from northwest to southeast (A to L) along the southern San Andreas Fault with location of surface fractures formed in response to 2010 El Mayor-Cucapah earthquake. Dashed line, San Andreas Fault; solid line, location of documented 2010 surface fractures. Amount of slip shown in millimeters for right-lateral (R) and vertical (V) components. Maps derived using selected contours from 1:24,000-scale topographic maps; location of fault from Clark (1984); location of strips shown in figure 1.

Figure 5. Photographs of fractures formed in response to the El Mayor-Cucapah earthquake and views of the San Andreas Fault in southeastern Coachella Valley. *A,* Fractures (black arrows) along San Andreas Fault in active wash between Thermal Canyon and Quarry Canyon; view to the northeast (see fig. 4, panel A–B for location). Photograph taken April 20, 2010, by K.J. Kendrick. *B,* Left-stepping fractures (black arrows) along San Andreas Fault in gravel road in Quarry Canyon. Photograph taken April 20, 2010, by K.J. Kendrick; view to the northwest. Green notebook in center of view for scale. *C,* View along San Andreas Fault (between white arrows) in Quarry Canyon; view to the southeast. Photograph taken April 20, 2010, by K.J. Kendrick. *D,* Oblique aerial view of San Andreas Fault (between white arrows) near Red Canyon; view to the west. Location of image shown in figure 4, panel B–C. Dark reddish-brown deposit beyond right white arrow is a sandy mudstone that was tectonically emplaced along this section of the San Andreas Fault. *E,* View along San Andreas Fault between Red Canyon and Painted Canyon; view to the southeast.

1987; the first of these was primary (coseismic) tectonic slip (Clark, 1972) and the second was slip triggered by the 1987 Superstition Hills earthquake (Hudnut and Clark, 1989). In 2010, discontinuous surface breaks formed along the Coyote Creek Fault over a distance of about 5 km (figs. 1, 6; table 1), at distances of 119–122 km from the El Mayor-Cucapah epicenter (table 1). The distribution and amounts of triggered slip were remarkably similar to those observed by Hudnut and Clark (1989) for the 1987 event. Breaks developed primarily in one broad area, immediately southeast of the Ocotillo Badlands (figs. 6, 7A–C) and in two, short isolated patches to the southeast (fig. 6). Displacements were small. Maximum measured dextral slip was only 16 mm. A feature of interest

that was seen during field studies is a mostly infilled, collapsed graben (fig. 7D). This feature is along the Coyote Creek Fault, but not in an area with new surface slip (fig. 6). Similar features were common along the Coyote Creek Fault following the 1968 Borrego Mountain earthquake (Clark, 1972).

Superstition Hills Fault

Field checks for surface breakage along the Superstition Hills Fault began 2 days after the El Mayor-Cucapah earthquake. Four of us (J.J.L., N.K., M.J.R., and B.P.E.O.) checked the fault on April 6–7, 2010. We mapped cracks

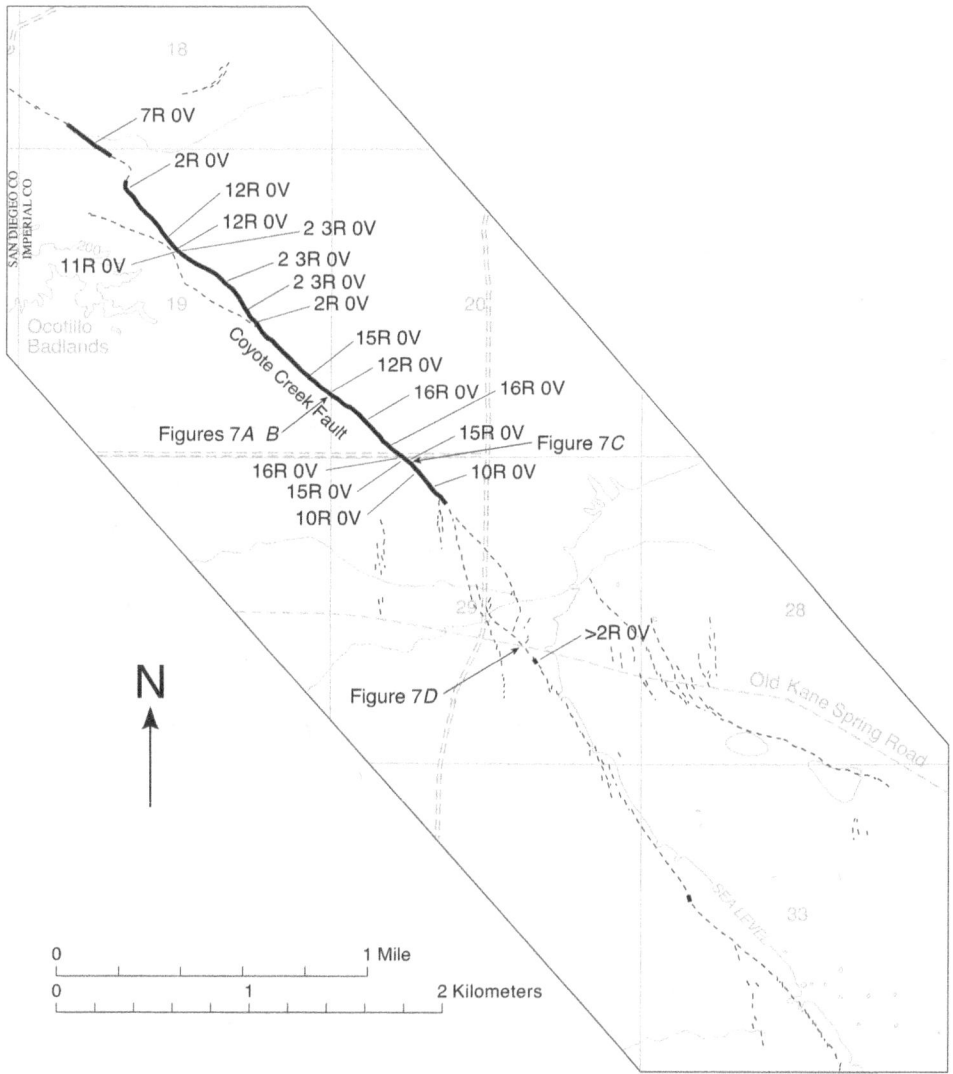

Figure 6. Strip map of central part of Coyote Creek Fault showing location of fractures formed in response to 2010 El Mayor-Cucapah earthquake (see fig. 1 for location of map area). Amount of slip shown in millimeters for right-lateral (R) and vertical (V) components. Map derived using selected contours from topographic maps; location of faults from Clark (1972). Map covers same section of Coyote Creek Fault as shown by Hudnut and Clark (1989).

and measured slip along about 23 km of the fault trace, at distances of about 79 and 99 km from the El Mayor-Cucapah epicenter to the southeast and northwest endpoints of observed triggered slip, respectively (table 1).

Surface slip in 2010 occurred on all three of the structural fault segments associated with the 1987 Superstition Hills earthquake (Sharp and others, 1989). Superstition Hills Fault segments are, from northwest to southeast, the north, central or Imler, and the Wienert strands (we discuss the Wienert

strand (fault) separately in this report). We mapped fresh breaks resulting from the 2010 El Mayor-Cucapah earthquake along most of the north strand and all of the central or Imler strand. Surface breaks in 2010 formed in uplifted Pleistocene lacustrine deposits.

Observed offset was small, less than 16 mm (figs. 8, 9A–C). The amount of dextral slip was largest near the southeastern end of the central or Imler strand (fig. 8). Locally, a small vertical component of slip was measured; nowhere did

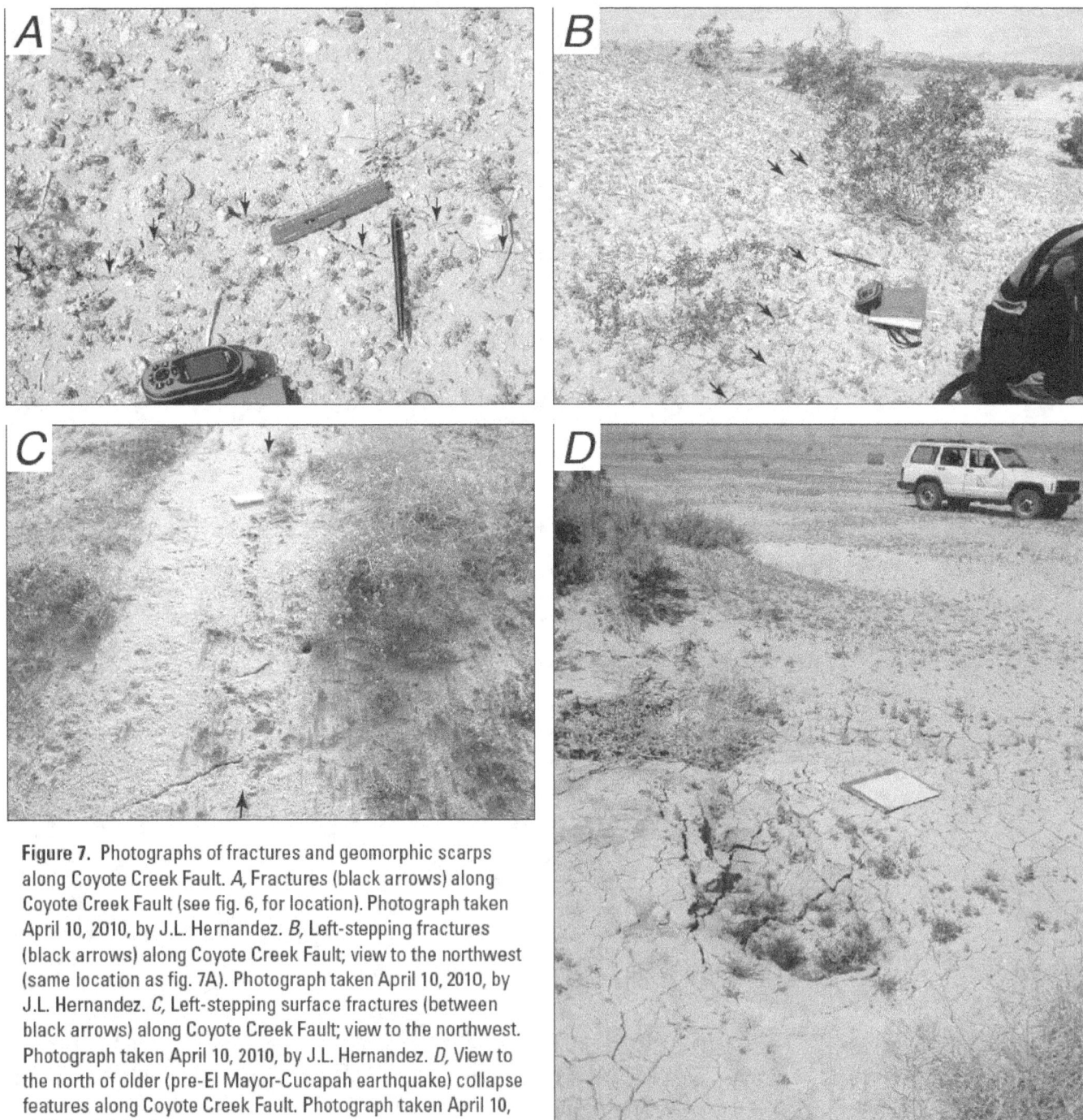

Figure 7. Photographs of fractures and geomorphic scarps along Coyote Creek Fault. *A,* Fractures (black arrows) along Coyote Creek Fault (see fig. 6, for location). Photograph taken April 10, 2010, by J.L. Hernandez. *B,* Left-stepping fractures (black arrows) along Coyote Creek Fault; view to the northwest (same location as fig. 7A). Photograph taken April 10, 2010, by J.L. Hernandez. *C,* Left-stepping surface fractures (between black arrows) along Coyote Creek Fault; view to the northwest. Photograph taken April 10, 2010, by J.L. Hernandez. *D,* View to the north of older (pre-El Mayor-Cucapah earthquake) collapse features along Coyote Creek Fault. Photograph taken April 10, 2010, by J.A. Treiman.

the vertical component exceed 3 mm. Where observed, the vertical component of slip was similar in relative proportions of scale and direction to that in previous episodes of triggered slip and in the 1987 primary surface faulting.

Discussion

There are five episodes of documented triggered surface slip (1968, 1979, 1981, 1992, and 1999) and 1987 primary surface faulting (Sharp and others, 1989) on the Superstition Hills Fault. The 1987 primary (coseismic) surface faulting was associated with an extended period of afterslip that began as more-or-less continuous aseismic slip and then decayed to episodic slip events (Bilham, 1989).

Timing of surface slip on the fault in 2010 is directly constrained by creepmeter measurements of slip (fig. 2). Surface slip at the site of the Superstition Hills creepmeter is a graphic example of greater slip amounts measured by creepmeters than on the nearby ground surface. Whereas the Superstition Hills creepmeter site measured about 23 mm of dextral slip, we measured only 16 mm of dextral slip (figs. 8, 9A). Again, the wider span of buried creepmeter instrumentation commonly records larger amounts of slip. In addition, a component of off-fault deformation may have been recorded by this creepmeter.

One of the most remarkable similarities between prior triggered slip events and the 2010 event is in the reoccupation of surface breakage localities. In each event, surface deformation recurred within a few centimeters of previous locations. Nail arrays and wooden-peg arrays placed across the Superstition Hills Fault following the 1987 primary surface faulting were offset by the El Mayor-Cucapah earthquake in exactly the same place as in 1987 and in intervening afterslip and triggered slip events. Figure 9D shows a site where slip was observed in 2010 and previous triggered slip events, all of which are superimposed on a preexisting fault scarp. At this location, the Superstition Hills Fault has juxtaposed different lithologies (siltstone against sandstone) that produce a pronounced vegetation lineament. Local, deep stream-cut exposures that cross the Superstition Hills Fault document the persistence of surface slip locations (fig. 9E).

The 2010 earthquake provided a new opportunity to carefully measure the distribution and amount of triggered surface slip within a structural stepover of the Superstition Hills Fault previously revealed by 1987 (tectonic) surface rupture (Sharp and others, 1989; Rymer, 1989). As with previous episodes of triggered slip, the 2010 surface breakage extended through the 50-m-wide structural stepover (see fig. 8, O–P). Detailed measurements of 2010 triggered slip in the stepover area show a decrease in slip on both north and central strands proximal to the stepover and only minor, 2–6 mm, dextral slip on individual strands extending past where slip is transferred from one strand to the other (fig. 8). Also, the 2010 triggered slip apparently transferred from one fault strand to the other in the same location where Rymer (1989)

had speculated that most of the 1987 primary slip transferred through the stepover (gray area in fig. 8, panel O–P).

Wienert Fault

Field checks for surface breakage along the Wienert Fault in the western Imperial Valley began 3 days after the El Mayor-Cucapah earthquake. Two of us (M.J.R. and B.P.E.O.) checked the Wienert Fault on April 7–8, 2010. Field checks were confined to paved and gravel roads and dirt shoulders of roads where the Wienert Fault broke the surface in 1987.

Discussion

Triggered slip in 2010 along the Wienert Fault in the western Imperial Valley occurred in the same location where the fault had moved tectonically in a previous moderate earthquake, the 1987 Superstition Hills event. We documented left-stepping, en echelon fractures crossing Wienert Road; the fractures extended into adjacent fields, where evidence of fresh fracturing was obscured by abundant desiccation cracks in the soil. We also checked for fresh surface fractures along Edgar Road and Worthington Road, to the northwest and southeast of Wienert Road, respectively (fig 10); however we did not observe fresh surface fractures along these roads.

Superstition Mountain Fault

Field checks for surface breakage along the Superstition Mountain Fault in the western Imperial Valley occurred on April 12, 2010, 8 days after the El Mayor-Cucapah earthquake. Three of us (M.J.R., J.L.H., and B.P.E.O.) examined the Superstition Mountain Fault trace on the northwestern end of Superstition Mountain, its central section, and on the southwest side of the mountain. We checked several fault scarps, but did not observe new slip associated with the El Mayor-Cucapah earthquake.

Kalin Fault

Field checks for surface breakage along the Kalin Fault in the northern Imperial Valley began 4 days after the El Mayor-Cucapah earthquake. Two of us (M.J.R. and B.P.E.O.) checked the Kalin Fault along two dirt roads crossing cultivated fields on April 8, 2010, and one of us (K.J.K.) made repeat observations on April 20, 2010. Field checks were limited to these two east-west-trending dirt roads, where the fault's location is known.

Discussion

Triggered slip in 2010 along the Kalin Fault in the northern Imperial Valley occurred in the same location

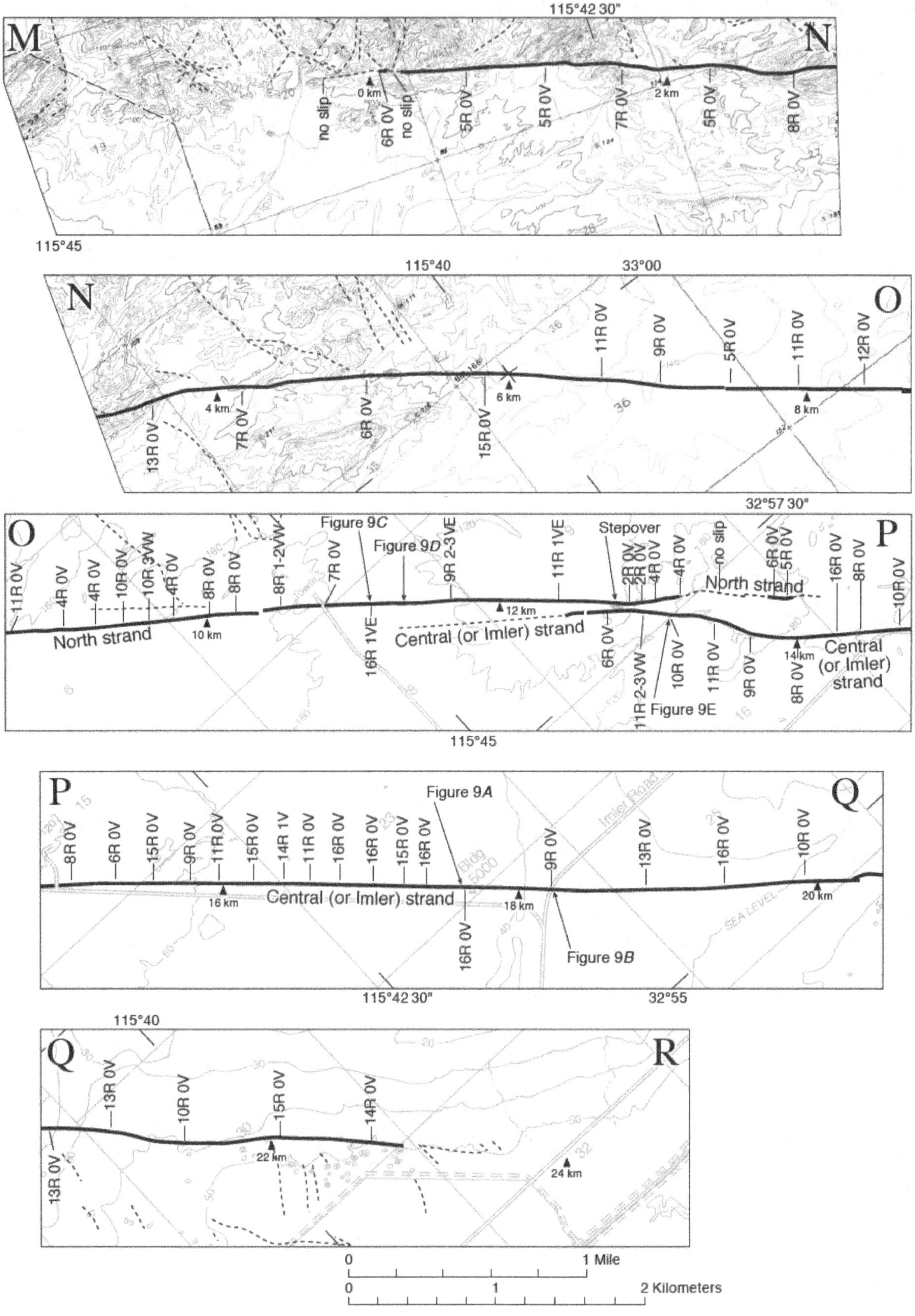
115°42 30"
M
N
no slip
0 km
6R 0V
no slip
5R 0V
5R 0V
7R 0V
2 km
5R 0V
8R 0V
115°45
115°40
33°00
N
O
11R 0V
9R 0V
5R 0V
11R 0V
12R 0V
4 km
6 km
8 km
13R 0V
7R 0V
6R 0V
15R 0V
32°57 30"
O
P
Figure 9C
Figure 9D
9R 2-3VE
11R 1VE
Stepover
no slip
11R 0V
4R 0V
4R 0V
10R 0V
10R 3VW
4R 0V
8R 0V
8R 0V
8R 1-2VW
7R 0V
2R 0V
2R 0V
4R 0V
4R 0V
6R 0V
5R 0V
16R 0V
8R 0V
10R 0V
North strand
12 km
10 km
North strand
Central (or Imler) strand
16R 1VE
6R 0V
11R 2-3VW
10R 0V
11R 0V
9R 0V
8R 0V
14 km
Central (or Imler) strand
Figure 9E
115°45
P
Q
Figure 9A
8R 0V
6R 0V
15R 0V
9R 0V
11R 0V
15R 0V
14R 1V
11R 0V
16R 0V
16R 0V
15R 0V
16R 0V
9R 0V
13R 0V
16R 0V
10R 0V
Imler Road
16 km
Central (or Imler) strand
18 km
20 km
SEA LEVEL
16R 0V
Figure 9B
115°42 30"
32°55
115°40
Q
R
13R 0V
10R 0V
15R 0V
14R 0V
13R 0V
22 km
24 km
0
1 Mile
0
1
2 Kilometers

where the fault had broken the surface during a swarm of microearthquakes in 2005 (Lohman and McGuire, 2007; Rymer, Hudnut, and Kendrick, unpublished work). The 2005 slip event resulted in a series of fault breaks about 170 m long that vertically offset a concrete-lined canal. Slip on the Kalin Fault manifests as nearly pure vertical slip. In 2005 the ground surface was freshly warped, if not also faulted, for a distance extending north-northeastward from the offset canal liner at least 800 m into an adjacent field of dense crops (figs. 11, 12B).

In 2010 we documented discontinuous surface breaks along the Kalin Fault over a distance of about 20 m (figs. 1, 11; table 1), at a distance of about 103 km from the El Mayor-Cucapah epicenter (table 1). Subtle breaks crossed one dirt road and its adjacent shoulder (fig. 11). Surface slip in 2010 likely extended farther, but local, dense vegetation (see upper part of fig 12B) prevented our observing the fresh fractures in the fields. Amounts of displacement were small; maximum measured vertical slip was only 3–5 mm, east side up. We did not see renewed breakage of the nearby concrete-lined canal, which had broken during the 2005 earthquake swarm.

High-resolution shallow seismic imaging across the Kalin Fault, both along the dirt road where fractures developed in 2005 and 2010 and along the dirt road near the top of figure 11, delineate a structurally complex fault in the subsurface. In the shallow subsurface (upper 200 m) along the more southerly of these two roads, Rymer and others (2009) interpret a narrow (10- to 30-m-wide) zone of faults that dips about 70 degrees to the northwest. Below 200 m depth the fault zone is nearly vertical, has a width of about 200 m, and consists of at least four anastomosing strands.

Imperial Fault

Our study of the Imperial Fault is restricted to that portion north of the U.S.-Mexico border (fig. 1). Field checks for surface breakage along the Imperial Fault began the day after the El Mayor-Cucapah earthquake. Two of us (M.J.R. and K.J.K.) checked the Imperial Fault at Harris Road on April 5, 2010; two of us (M.J.R. and B.P.E.O.) returned to the Imperial Fault for more extensive documentation of the fault on April 8–9, 2010. Field checks were made primarily along roadways and dirt shoulders that cross the fault; mapping and measurements were made predominantly on dirt shoulders of roads. Much of the fault crosses uncultivated fields; however, we walked along the fault trace only locally.

Discontinuous surface breaks formed along the Imperial Fault over a distance of about 22 km (figs. 13, 14; table 1), at distances of about 52 and 73 km from the El Mayor-Cucapah epicenter to the northwest and southeast endpoints of the triggered slip, respectively (table 1). Two factors limited the continuity and extent of our mapping of surface breakage. Cultivated fields, especially fields with dense crops, were not checked for surface fractures. Some fields recently had been cleared of crops, and these were checked for surface breaks. Generally this was a futile effort because locally abundant desiccation cracks masked the presence of small slip displacements. The 2010 triggered slip likely extended farther north than Harris Road. No slip was observed at Keystone Road, and thus, the northern end of 2010 triggered slip lies somewhere between Harris and Keystone Roads, north of our measurement sites (fig. 13, panel V–W).

Offset values were small, dextral slip being less than 16 mm (figs. 13, 14B). Dextral slip was greatest near the northern end of triggered surface breakage (fig. 13). Locally there was a minor 1–5 mm) vertical component of slip; larger amounts of vertical slip (as much as 20 mm) occurred in Mesquite basin (near kilometers 23–24, fig. 13), where fault scarps indicate oblique slip for this part of the Imperial Fault (fig. 14A).

Discussion

The Imperial Fault has a rich history of documented surface slips. Primary surface faulting is associated with moderate to large earthquakes in 1940 (M7.1) and 1979 (M6.4) and small earthquakes in 1966 (M3.6) and 1975 (M4.2); triggered slip occurred in 1968, 1981, 1987, 1999, and 2010; and there have been many earthquake swarms and minor aseismic creep events along the fault (Goulty and others, 1978; Louie and others, 1985; Cohn and others, 1982; Sharp, 1989; Lyons and others, 2002). Afterslip associated with the 1979 earthquake continued episodically for years after that event (Sharp and others, 1982). In addition, an earthquake on the Superstition Hills Fault in 1971 also triggered slip along the Imperial Fault (Allen and others 1972).

Timing of slip events on the Imperial Fault within the Imperial Valley is directly constrained only by the time of repeated field reconnaissance. The freshness of breaks seen on the Imperial Fault along Harris Road the day after the earthquake suggests that these surface breaks were triggered by the 2010 El Mayor-Cucapah earthquake.

 Figure 8. Strip maps of Superstition Hills Fault with location of surface fractures formed in response to 2010 El Mayor-Cucapah earthquake (see fig. 1 for location of panels M–R). Dotted line, Superstition Hills Fault and related faults; solid line, location of documented 2010 surface fractures. Amount of slip shown in millimeters for both right-lateral (R) and vertical (V) components. Vertical component of slip, where present, is indicated with either west (W) or east (E) side up. Map strips derived using selected contours from topographic maps. Distance scale along fault is the same as used by Sharp and others (1986a, 1989), with reference point located near western end of Superstition Hills Fault.

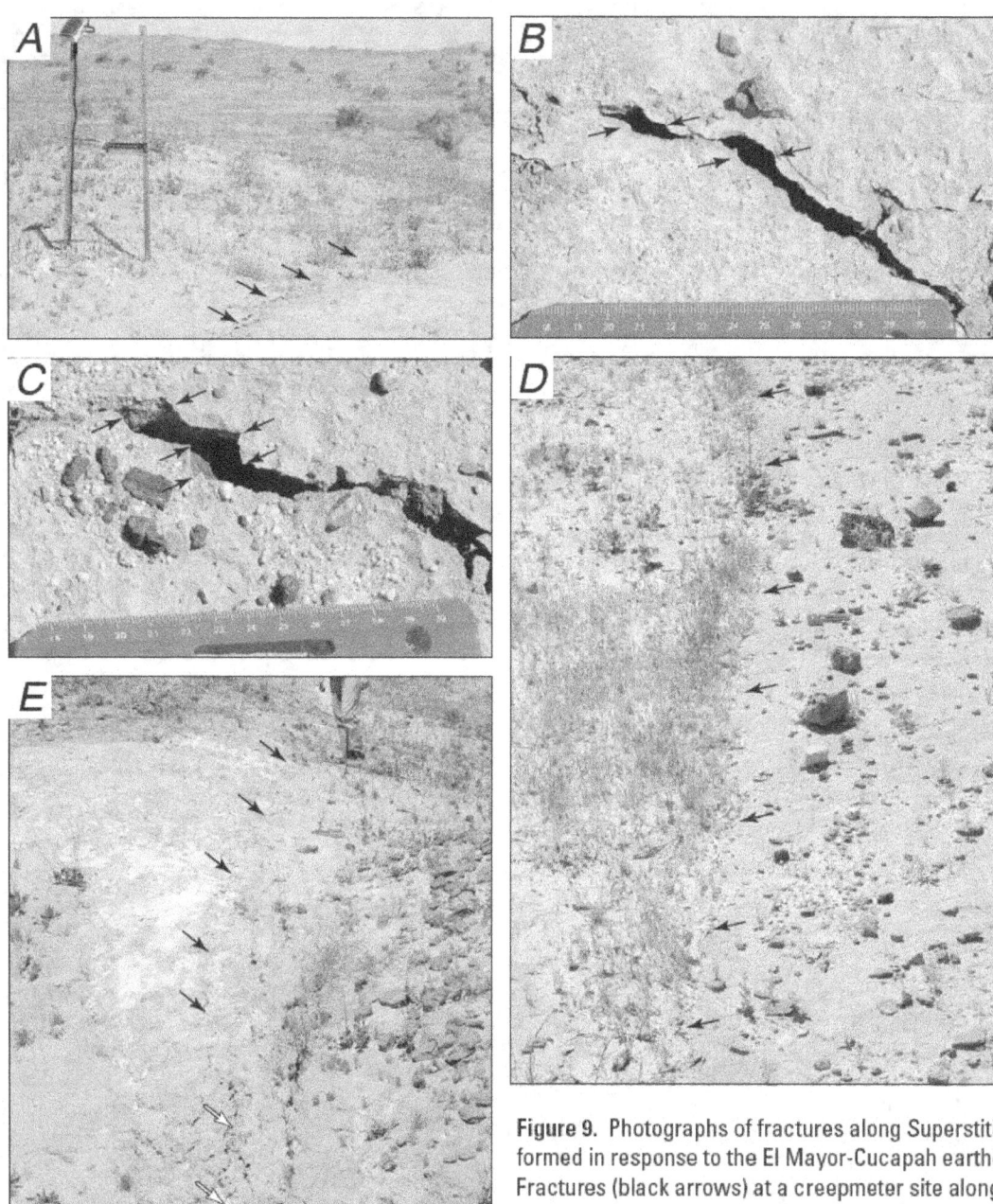

Figure 9. Photographs of fractures along Superstition Hills Fault formed in response to the El Mayor-Cucapah earthquake. *A,* Fractures (black arrows) at a creepmeter site along Superstition Hills Fault (see fig. 8 for location). Photograph taken April 8, 2010. *B,* Fractures along Superstition Hills Fault. Black arrows mark matches across en echelon fractures; scale in centimeters. Photograph taken April 11, 2010. *C,* Fractures along Superstition Hills Fault. Black arrows mark matches across en echelon fractures. *D,* Fractures (black arrows) along Superstition Hills Fault; view to the southeast. The fault has juxtaposed relatively clay-rich and sand-rich strata from the same mid-Pleistocene sedimentary sequence, the transition expressed as a vegetation lineament. Photograph taken April 8, 2010. *E,* Fractures (black arrows) along Superstition Hills Fault where ground surface is cut by a gulley. Fractures (white arrows) continue into near-vertical gulley exposure, where Quaternary fault (see label) is visible; view to the northwest. Photograph taken April 8, 2010.

As with the San Andreas and Superstition Hills Faults, the location of surface breakage in 2010 along individual traces of the Imperial Fault closely matches the location of earlier triggered slip and primary surface rupture. Fresh surface breaks, where they occurred, formed in exactly the same place as previous slip features. In fact, both right-oblique slip and pure dextral slip recur in previously documented locations. Figure 14 shows a variety of locations with evidence of repeated slip, both in historical and geologic time. Figure 14A shows evidence of recurrent movement along the Imperial Fault near the base of a prominent scarp at Harris Road and along the southwest margin of Mesquite Basin (see fig. 1). Although surface rupture shown in figure 14A occurred in 1979, subsequent triggered slip events occurred in 1981, 1987, and 1999 at exactly the same location. In fact, figure 14B shows surface fractures that occurred in association with the 2010 El Mayor-Cucapah earthquake along the same persistent fault scarp.

Other examples of the recurrent movement of the fault and persistence in location of rupture or fracturing are shown in figures 14C–F. Fresh fractures across the ground surface and within an open paleoseismic trench exposure (of R. Tsang, A. Meltzner, and T. Rockwell) align with the fault plane in the near surface at this location along the Imperial Fault (fig. 14C). Figure 14D shows surface expression and evidence of tectonic offset from the 1940 and 1979 earthquakes and their respective afterslips. This 2009 view to the west along Evan Hewes Highway shows the cumulative slip where the fault crosses the pavement. Unfortunately for geologic investigations, this roadway was repaved in the months before the 2010 El Mayor-Cucapah earthquake. The photograph was taken in March 2009, and a subsequent visit to the site revealed the same scene in June 2009. Movement on the Imperial Fault (identified by white arrows on the sides of the photo) has offset the center paving joint (center of road on distant side of fault and white arrow in bottom-left of image). We did not observe fresh surface fractures at this location following the El Mayor-Cucapah earthquake. This is consistent with other, nearby observations of no new slip. However, Interstate 8 was offset in 2010 (fig. 14E, F). We measured surface fractures on the northern frontage road of I-8 (to the left in fig. 14E; fig. 13, panel Y–Z). Figure 14F shows approximately the same area as figure 14E but is a vertical aerial view taken immediately after the 1979 Imperial Valley

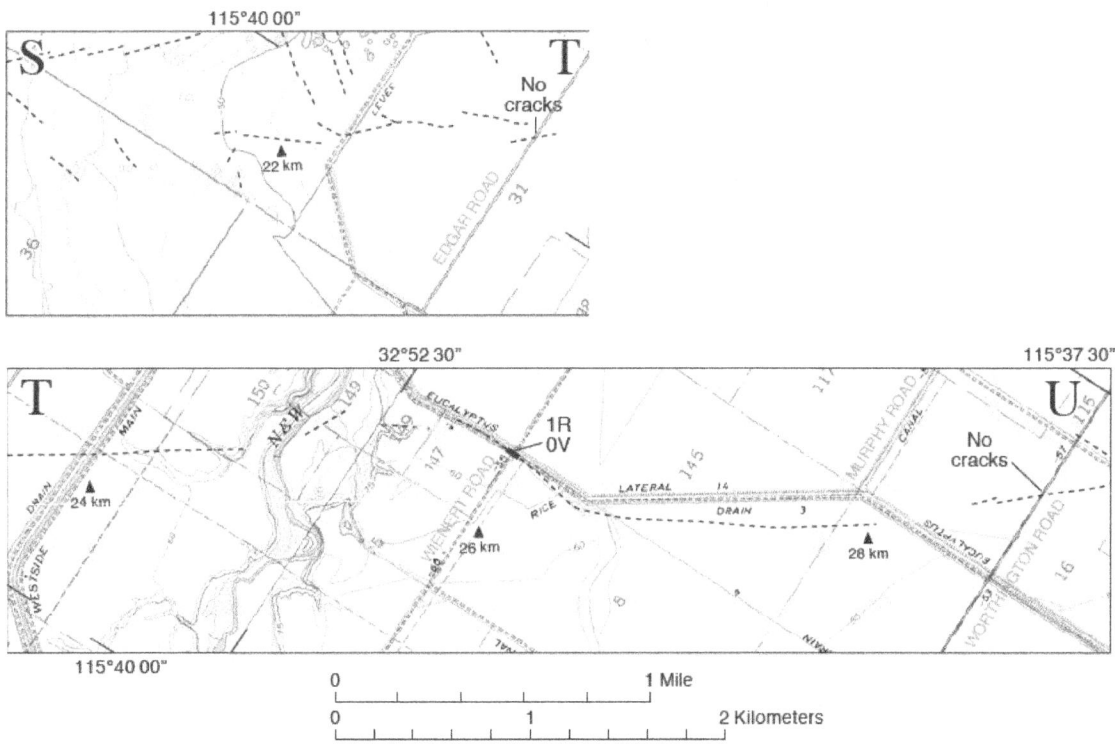

Figure 10. Strip maps of Wienert Fault (Wienert strand of the Superstition Hills Fault) with location of surface fractures formed in response to 2010 El Mayor-Cucapah earthquake (see fig. 1 for location of panels S–U). Dotted line, Wienert Fault; solid line, location of documented 2010 surface fractures. Amount of slip shown in millimeters for both right-lateral (R) and vertical (V) components. Map strips derived from topographic maps. Distance scale along fault is the same as used by Sharp and others (1989), with reference point located near western end of Superstition Hills Fault.

earthquake. This section of I-8 was paved just before the 1979 earthquake and, although the roadway is broken, there was little displacement. Most of the total (that is, coseismic and postseismic) offset associated with the 1979 earthquake developed as afterslip (Sharp and others, 1982).

Brawley Fault Zone

Field checks for surface breakage along the Brawley Fault Zone in the central Imperial Valley began 4 days after

the El Mayor-Cucapah earthquake. Two of us (M.J.R. and B.P.E.O.) checked the Brawley Fault Zone (figs. 1, 15) on April 8, 2010. Field checks were made along paved roads and their dirt shoulders, and locally along drainage ditches.

Discussion

Triggered slip in 2010 along the Brawley Fault Zone in the central Imperial Valley occurred where it had in previous moderate to large earthquakes. The two previous documented

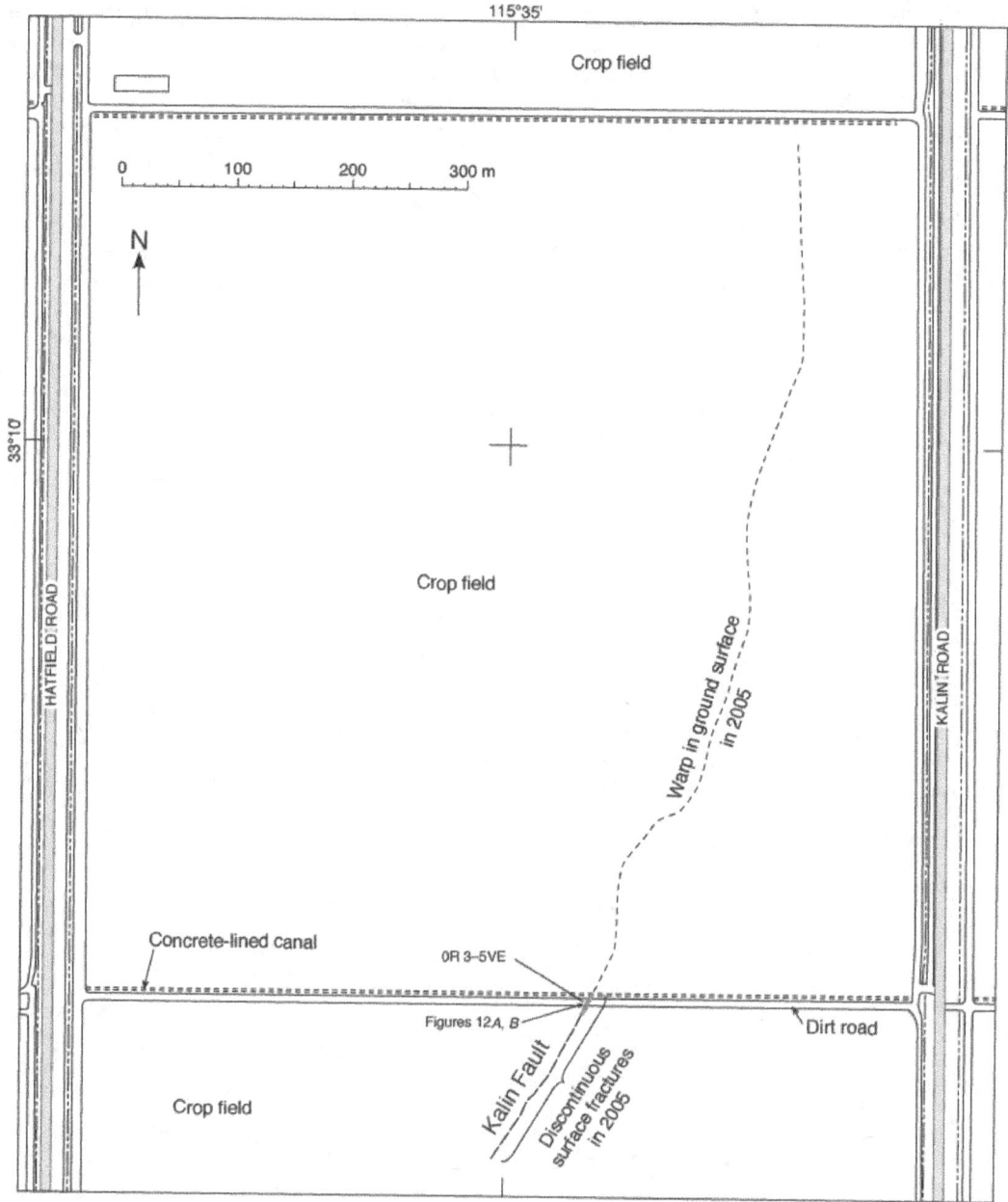

Figure 11. Map of Kalin Fault with location of surface fractures formed in association with 2010 El Mayor-Cucapah earthquake (see fig. 1 for location of map).

slip events, in 1975 and 1979, were associated with primary, tectonic slip; the former from the 1975 Brawley swarm and the latter from the 1979 Imperial Valley earthquake (Sharp, 1976; Sharp and others, 1982; see also Meltzner and others, 2006, for discussion of prior fault activity). Figures 16A–D show fresh surface fractures along the Brawley Fault Zone following the El Mayor-Cucapah earthquake.

Discontinuous surface breaks formed along much of the length of the Brawley Fault Zone. Surface slip in 2010 was visible over a distance of about 13 km (figs. 1, 15; table 1), at distances of about 66 and 78 km from the El Mayor-Cucapah epicenter to the southern and northern endpoints of triggered slip, respectively (table 1). Maximum measured slip values were about 20 mm for the vertical component of slip and about 13 mm for the horizontal right-lateral component. Locally, fresh surface fractures broke concrete canal liners, which were already being patched when we visited the fault zone.

Faults in the Yuha Desert Area

Field checks for surface breakage along faults in the Yuha Desert area of southwestern Imperial Valley (figs. 1, 17) began 1 day after the El Mayor-Cucapah earthquake. Repeat visits to the area were made in April, May, June, and August 2010. Given the structural complexity of the area and the great number of faults, both mapped and previously unrecognized, we discuss our investigations in a geographically segmented, generally east-to-west order. We start with descriptions of our studies and faults observed, beginning along the U.S.-Mexico border on the western edge of the cultivated areas of the Imperial Valley (see figs. 17, 18). From there, we progress westerly (figs. 19–26), then step north and again progress from east to west (figs. 17, 27–34). Another northward step in our

presentation brings us to the northern reaches of triggered slips in the Yuha Desert area and to the southeasternmost (mapped) extent of the Elsinore Fault Zone (see figs. 17, 35–36).

Methods used in the Yuha Desert area were similar to those stated in the "Methods" section above, with a few additional details. Our initial fieldwork in this area focused on surveys of faults on existing maps. We also drove along gravel roads in the area, which resulted in finding what we describe below as the Yuha Fault, one of the significant faults that slipped in California in the El Mayor-Cucapah earthquake sequence. We also studied pre-2010 aerial imagery, such as the NAIP (National Agriculture Imagery Program) digital orthophoto coverage, as a means to locate other possible previously unrecognized faults. This approach also yielded positive results, but was time consuming, given all the subtle fault traces in the area, only a few of which moved in the 2010 event. The approach that proved most rewarding was to use interferograms prepared by NASA's Uninhabited Aerial Vehicle Synthetic Aperture Radar (UAVSAR) to map surface dislocations, then find these sites in the field for visual verification and fault-displacement measurements. However, the interferograms were received in mid-June, well after field crews and cooler field conditions had left the area. The UAVSAR imagery indicated that dozens of faults of various lengths throughout the Yuha Desert area had moved in this event. Despite several return trips to the field to verify the UAVSAR-identified fault dislocations, there still are many faults that we have not had the time or resources to document in the field. Thus, as shown in figure 17 and the following detailed maps (figs. 18, 19, 21, 23, 25, 27, 29, 31, 33, and 35), we distinguish faults with field-verified displacements (red lines) from faults with dislocations inferred from UAVSAR interferograms (orange lines). Some orange lines include short red sections where we "spot checked" our mapping

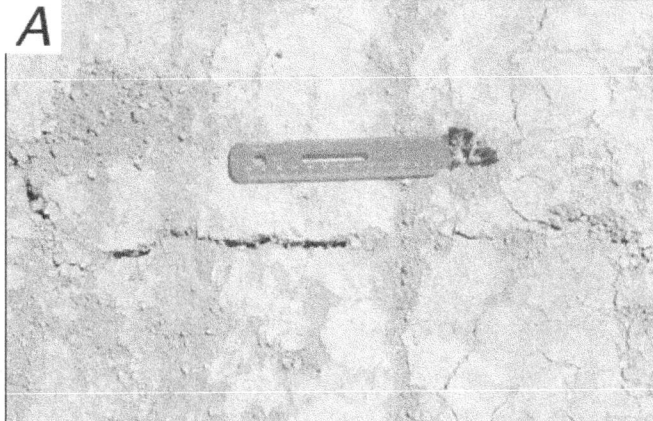

Figure 12. Photographs of Kalin Fault and surface fractures formed in response to the 2010 El Mayor-Cucapah earthquake. *A*, Vertical view of fractures with 14-cm-long scale. *B*, View of fractures across dirt roadway. Concrete canal liner (at top of photo) was not broken by new fractures. Photographs taken April 10, 2010.

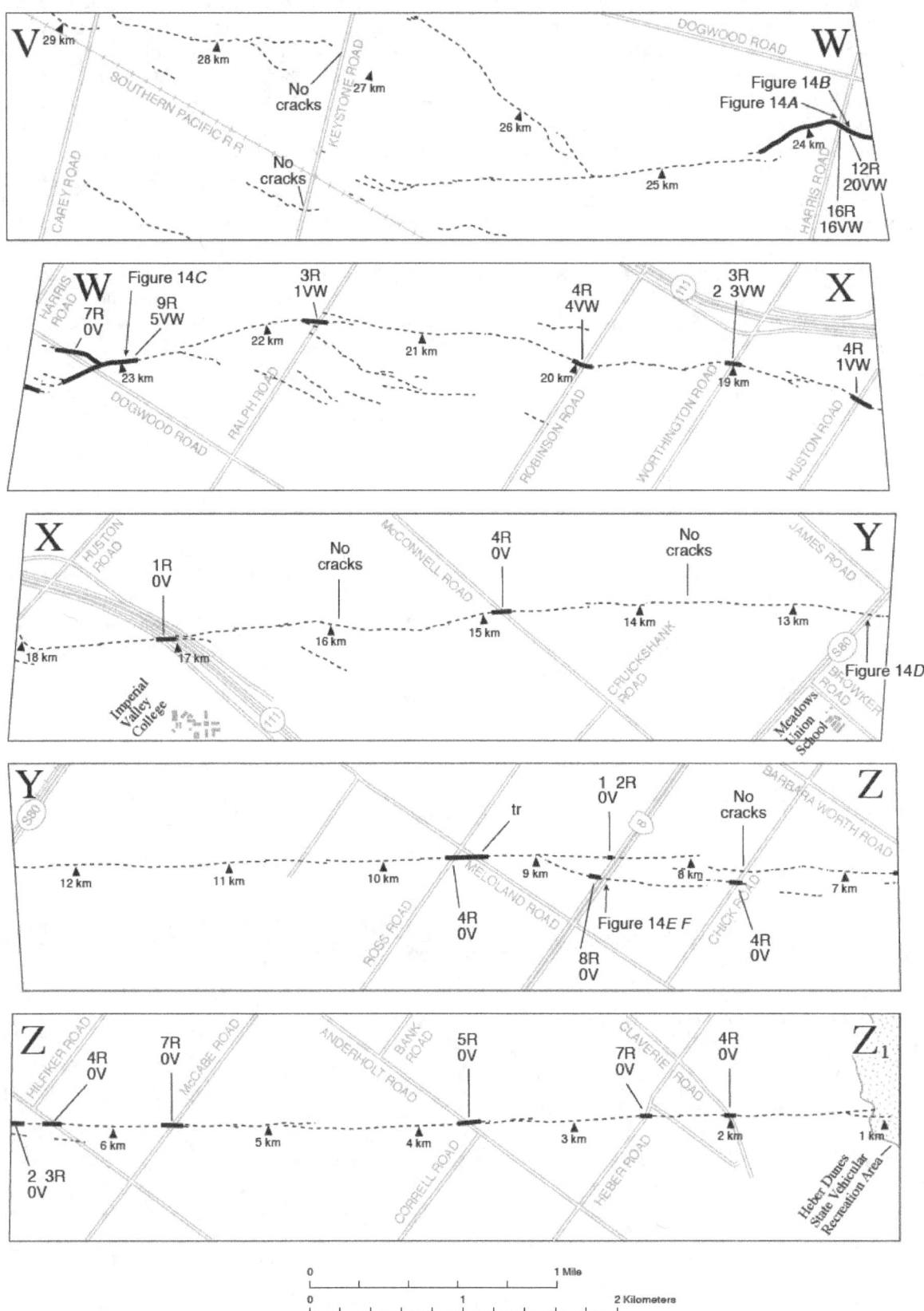

Figure 13. Strip maps of Imperial Fault with location of surface fractures formed in response to 2010 El Mayor-Cucapah earthquake (see fig. 1 for location of panels V–Z$_1$). Dotted line, Imperial Fault; solid line, location of documented 2010 surface fractures. Amount of slip shown in millimeters for both right-lateral (R) and vertical (V) components. Vertical component of slip, where present, is indicated with either west (W) or east (E) side up. Map strips depict local roads from 7 1/2-minute topographic maps. Distance scale along fault is the same as used by Sharp and others (1982), with reference point located near southern end of Imperial Fault.

Figure 14. Photographs of surface fractures and long-term offset of features along the Imperial Fault. *A*, Aerial photograph of the Imperial Fault at Harris Road. Photograph taken October 1979, shortly after the 1979 Imperial Valley earthquake. View to the southwest. *B*, Locally continuous, right-oblique surface fractures along Imperial Fault; view to the southwest. Photograph taken about 70 m south of Harris Road; photograph shows about 4 meters of surface fractures. Photograph taken April 5, 2010. *C*, Right-lateral surface fractures along Imperial Fault across and through a paleoseismic trench exposure. Photograph shows surface fractures (black arrows) and fresh fractures in a vertical exposure in the trench wall (white arrows), along edge of long-term Imperial Fault; view to the south. Photograph taken April 11, 2010. *D*, Right-lateral fault offset at Evan Hewes Highway due to recurrent movement on the Imperial Fault. View to the west. Photograph taken March 12, 2009; roadway was resurfaced some time between June 2009 and April 2010. *E*, Right-lateral fault offset at I-8 due to recurrent movement on the Imperial Fault; view to the east. Photograph taken April 11, 2010. *F*, Vertical aerial photograph of the Imperial Fault and I-8, showing two fault traces (between white arrows) in a structural stepover (compare with fault map in fig. 13). North is at top in this view. Photograph taken October 16, 1979.

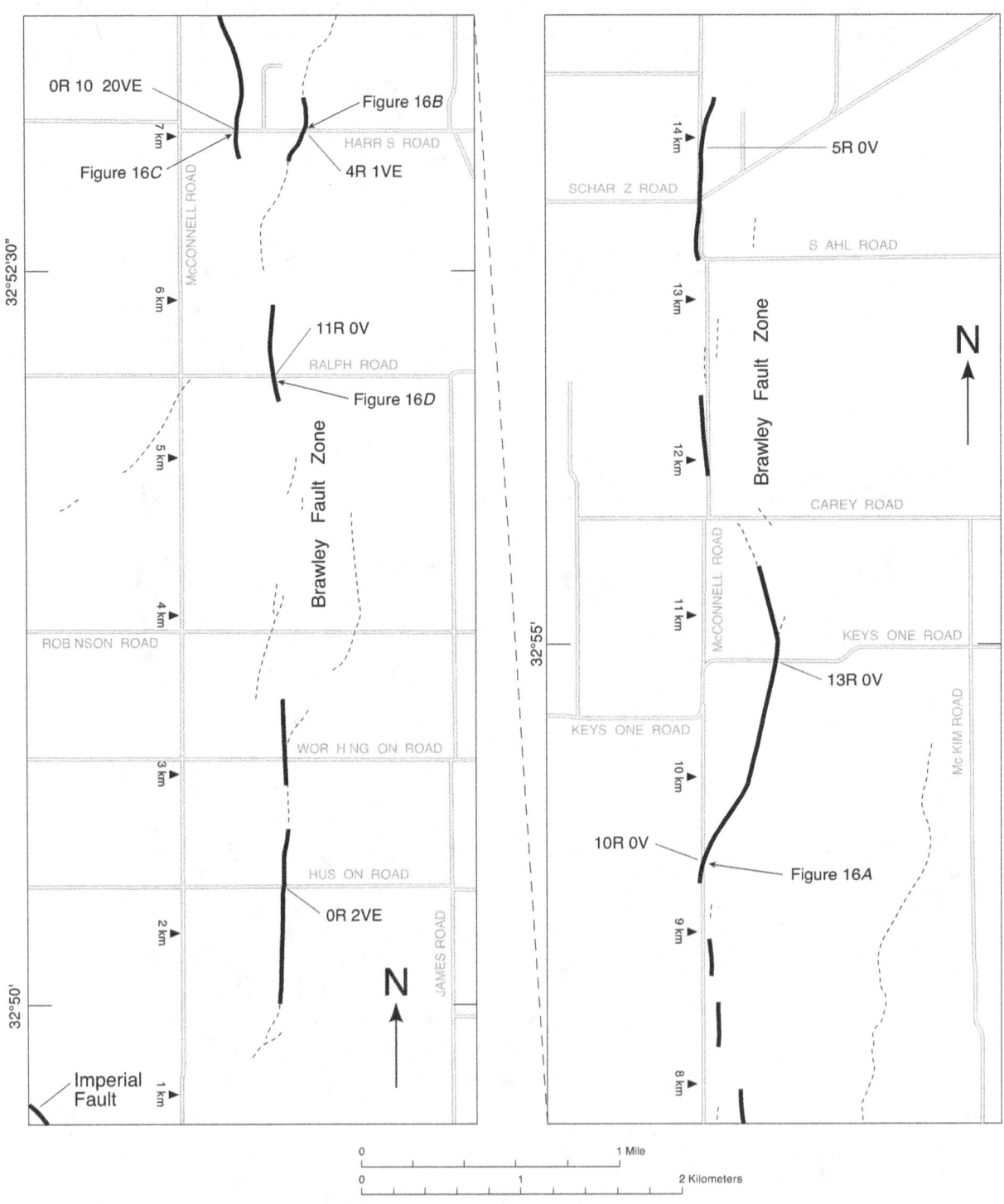

Figure 15. Strip maps of Brawley Fault Zone with location of surface fractures formed in response to 2010 El Mayor-Cucapah earthquake (see fig. 1 for location of map strips). Dotted line, Brawley Fault Zone; solid line, location of documented 2010 surface fractures. Amount of slip shown in millimeters for both right-lateral (R) and vertical (V) components. Vertical component of slip, where present, indicated with either west (W) or east (E) side up. Map strips depict local roads from Holtville West and Alamorio 7 1/2-minute topographic maps. Distance scale along fault is the same as used by Sharp and others (1982), with reference point located near southern end of Imperial Fault.

Figure 16. Photographs of surface fractures along Brawley Fault Zone in response to the 2010 El Mayor-Cucapah earthquake. *A,* Surface fractures (black arrows) along Brawley Fault Zone and across McConnell Road; view to the southwest. Photograph taken April 9, 2010. *B,* Close-up view of fresh surface fractures along Brawley Fault Zone in shoulder of Harris Road; scale in centimeters. Photograph taken April 9, 2010. *C,* Left-stepping, fractures (black arrows) along Brawley Fault Zone and across shoulder of Harris Road; view to the north. Photograph taken April 9, 2010. *D,* Fresh surface fractures (black arrows) along Brawley Fault Zone and across Ralph Road; view to the north. Slight vertical component of slip (2 mm, up on east [right] side) more noticeable at white arrow. Photograph taken April 9, 2010.

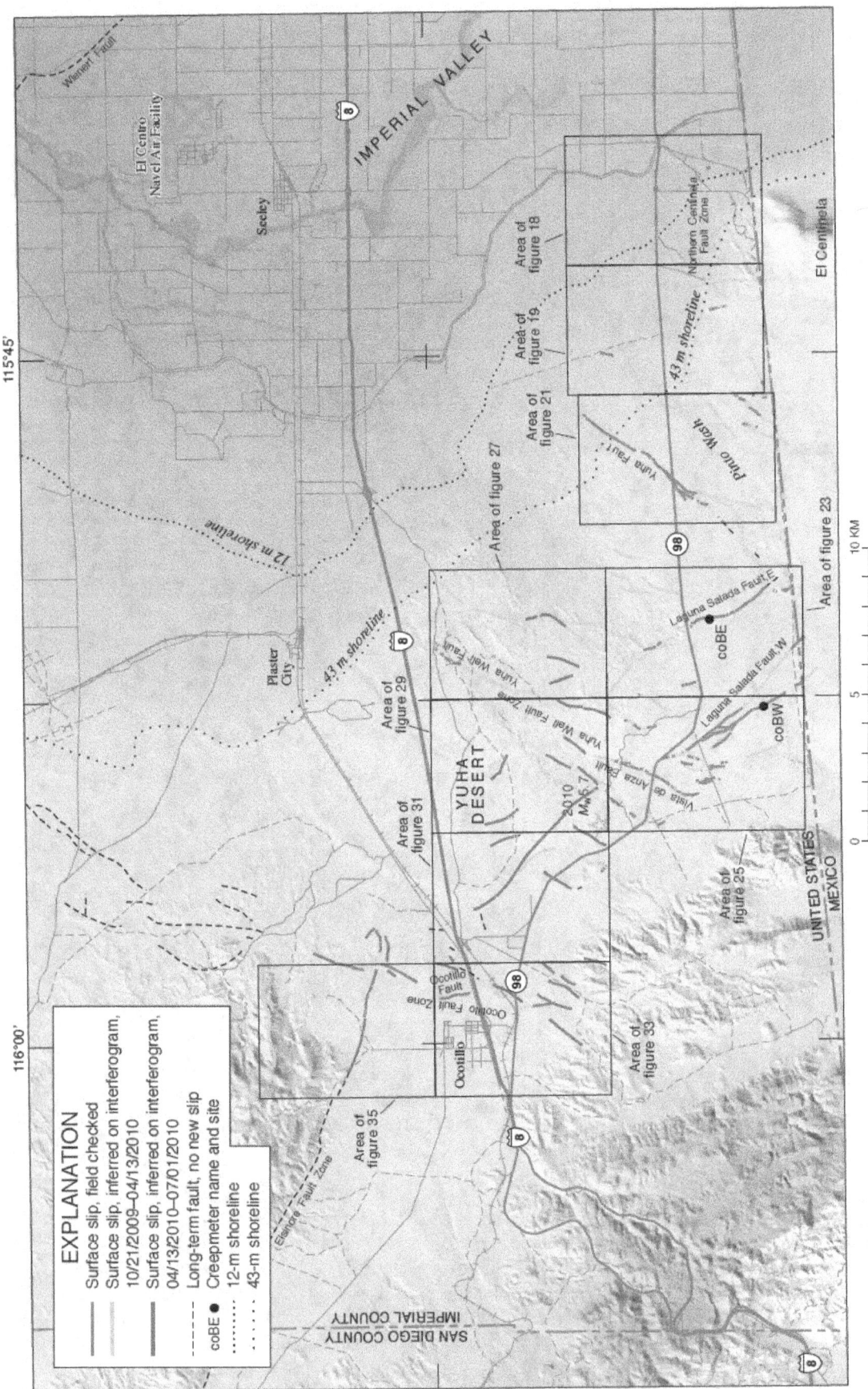

Figure 17. Shaded-relief map with background of roads, towns, and faults in the greater Yuha Desert area (see fig. 1 for location of map); also shown are areas of figs. 18, 19, 21, 23, 25, 27, 29, 31, 33, and 35. Red lines, field-verified surface fractures; orange lines, location of surface fractures inferred from dislocations in UAVSAR interferograms. Orange star, location of M_w 5.7 aftershock epicenter. Highstand of ancient Lake Cahuilla (12-m shoreline) and an earlier lake (43-m shoreline) are shown with dotted lines. Black dots show the location of creepmeter stations.

of dislocations on interferograms with field visits. Time constraints precluded verifying all inferred UAVSAR fault movements in the field.

The following descriptions of faults and fault zones are mainly limited to new surface breakage. That is, in this report we concentrate on triggered slip. Discussions about long-term activity of various faults, possible fault interactions, or paleoseismic histories are beyond the scope of this report. However, we do note that while mapping fresh surface slip we also saw many faults with no evidence of surface slip during the El Mayor-Cucapah earthquake sequence.

Included in figure 17 are the location of former shorelines of ancient Lake Cahuilla (12-m shoreline) and an earlier lake (43-m shoreline). For discussion of ancient lakes in the region and their highstand locations, see Blake (1854; 1915), Stanley (1963; 1966), Thomas (1963), Van de Kamp (1973), and Waters (1983). We have added lake highstands to the figure because wave action at these shorelines, and at lower elevations as the lakes receded, acted as erosive agents that removed or modified subtle fault scarps. Hence, evidence of preexisting fault scarps is subdued, but still present, below the two highstands.

Northern Centinela Fault Zone

A group of generally north-trending right-lateral and left-lateral faults are herein named the Northern Centinela Fault Zone (fig. 17). Faults within this zone extend northward from El Centinela, Mexico (known as 'Mount Signal' in the United States), the namesake for the fault zone. Individual fault traces within the fault zone in California are about 1.2–2.6 km long.

Field checks for surface breakage in the Northern Centinela Fault Zone (figs. 17–19) began on May 12, 2010, 38 days after the El Mayor-Cucapah earthquake. One of us (J.A.T.) checked the Northern Centinela Fault Zone in its westernmost extent (figs. 17, 19) and found minor, fresh surface slip. Additional field checks were made on June 19, 2010, in the broader fault zone (J.A.T.) based on dislocations on interferograms. In this latter field venture we checked and verified surface slip along additional faults within the Northern Centinela Fault Zone (fig. 18). Unfortunately, some recent surface slip likely had already been obscured by active aeolian sand deposition since the earthquake.

Discussion

Triggered slip in 2010 along faults within the Northern Centinela Fault Zone was small. Minor amounts of lateral slip were seen along sections of faults within the fault zone. Field evidence for the presence of active faults in the Northern Centinela Fault Zone is weak, especially at ancient lake highstands and lower elevations, where wave action from receding lake levels likely eroded subtle fault scarps. One exception is the westernmost fault within the fault zone (the approximately north-south fault in the center of Section 22,

fig. 19), which has an obvious fault scarp that extends at least 3.4 km south of the U.S.-Mexico border. More prominent surface slip is reported south of the border (Sinan Akciz, written commun., 2010, 2011; Fletcher and others, 2010).

Faults South of Pinto Wash

We found and mapped fresh surface fractures in a small group of northeast-trending left-lateral faults south of Pinto Wash (figs. 17, 19–22B). Individual faults in the group (within California) are about 1.0–1.5 km long. Field checks for surface breakage on faults in this group occurred on June 18, 2010. Two of us (J.A.T. and M.J.R.) checked faults in the area and found minor, fresh surface slip.

Discussion

Triggered slip in 2010 along faults south of Pinto Wash was expressed as discontinuous to continuous breaks, the latter being most common. Measured left-lateral slip values ranged from about 10 to about 40 mm (fig. 22A). Field evidence for the presence of faults south of Pinto Wash ranged from weak fault scarps (fig. 20) to cemented shear zones (fig. 22B). Outcrop patterns suggest some bedding-plane control on the fault location. Details of this latter possibility are beyond the scope of this report, but would be of interest for future fault studies.

Yuha Fault

Field checks of surface breakage along a previously unrecognized northeast-trending, left-lateral fault in the Yuha Desert began two days after the El Mayor-Cucapah earthquake. Herein we name this fault the Yuha Fault, for the nearby bench mark "Yuha" (fig. 21). Three of us (M.J.R., J.A.T., and K.J.K.) checked the Yuha Fault in the areas both north and south of State Highway 98 (figs. 17, 21) on April 6 and 7, 2010. Field checks were also made farther south of the initial mapping (by J.A.T., P.J.I., and J.L.H.) on April 9–11, 2010. Further field checks of aerial photographic lineaments northwest of previously mapped fault breakage and north of State Highway 98 were made on May 11 and 12 (J.A.T. and K.J.K.) and again on May 27, 2010 (M.J.R.). The Yuha Fault is about 5–7 km long and, locally, has a subtle to well-expressed fault scarp (figs. 22B, C).

Discussion

Triggered slip in 2010 along the Yuha Fault not only revealed the presence of the fault, but also demonstrated some of the longest, most continuous surface breakage (5–7 km) and indicated a more complicated prior slip history relative to other faults in the Yuha Desert area. The Yuha Fault also had larger slip displacements than other faults visited in the field. We

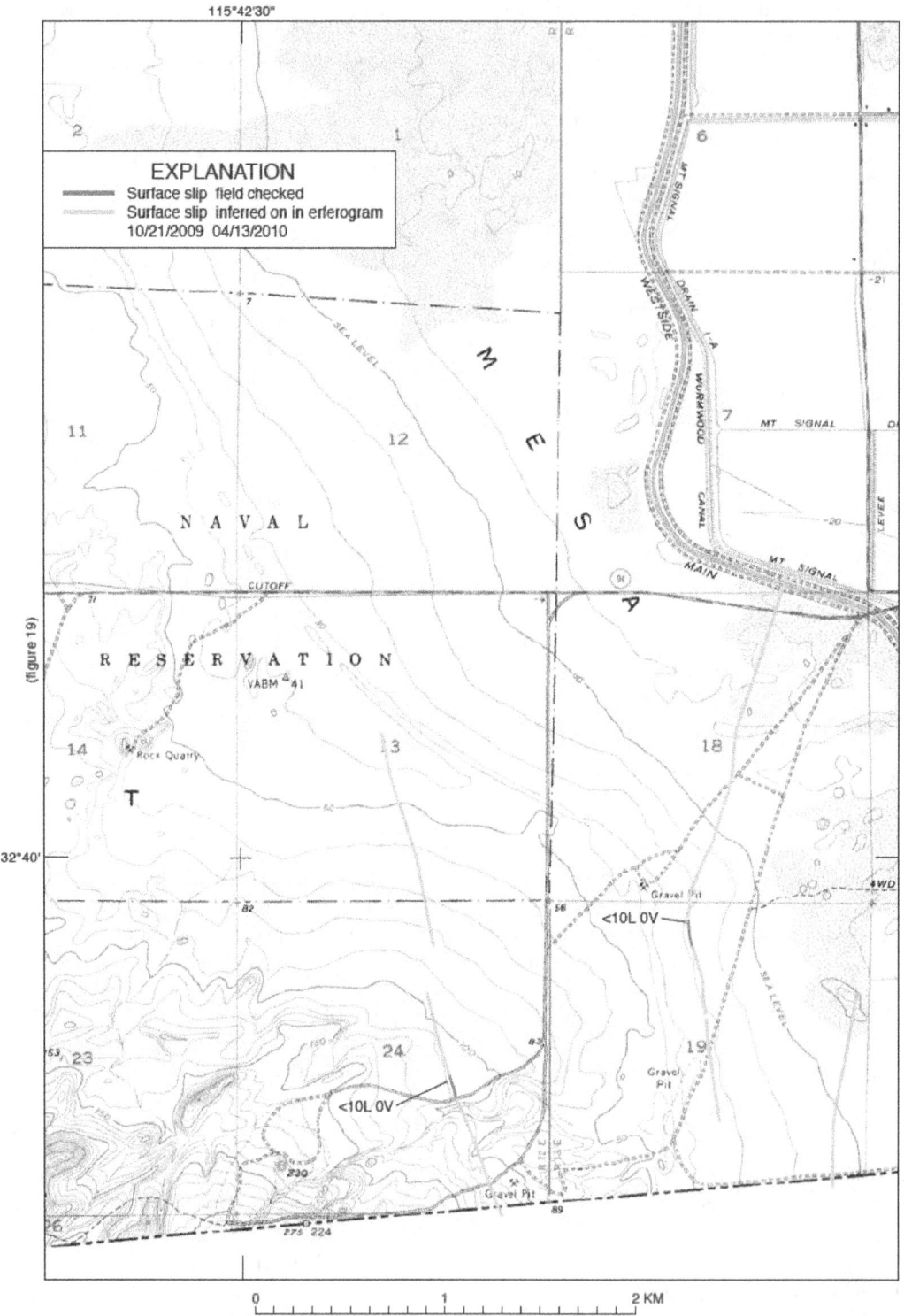

Figure 18. Map of faults and surface fractures in easternmost Yuha Desert. Faults shown are part of the Northern Centinela Fault Zone. Amount of slip shown in millimeters for both left-lateral (L) and vertical (V) components. Map base from a portion of the Mount Signal 7 1/2-minute topographic quadrangle. See figure 17 for location of map area.

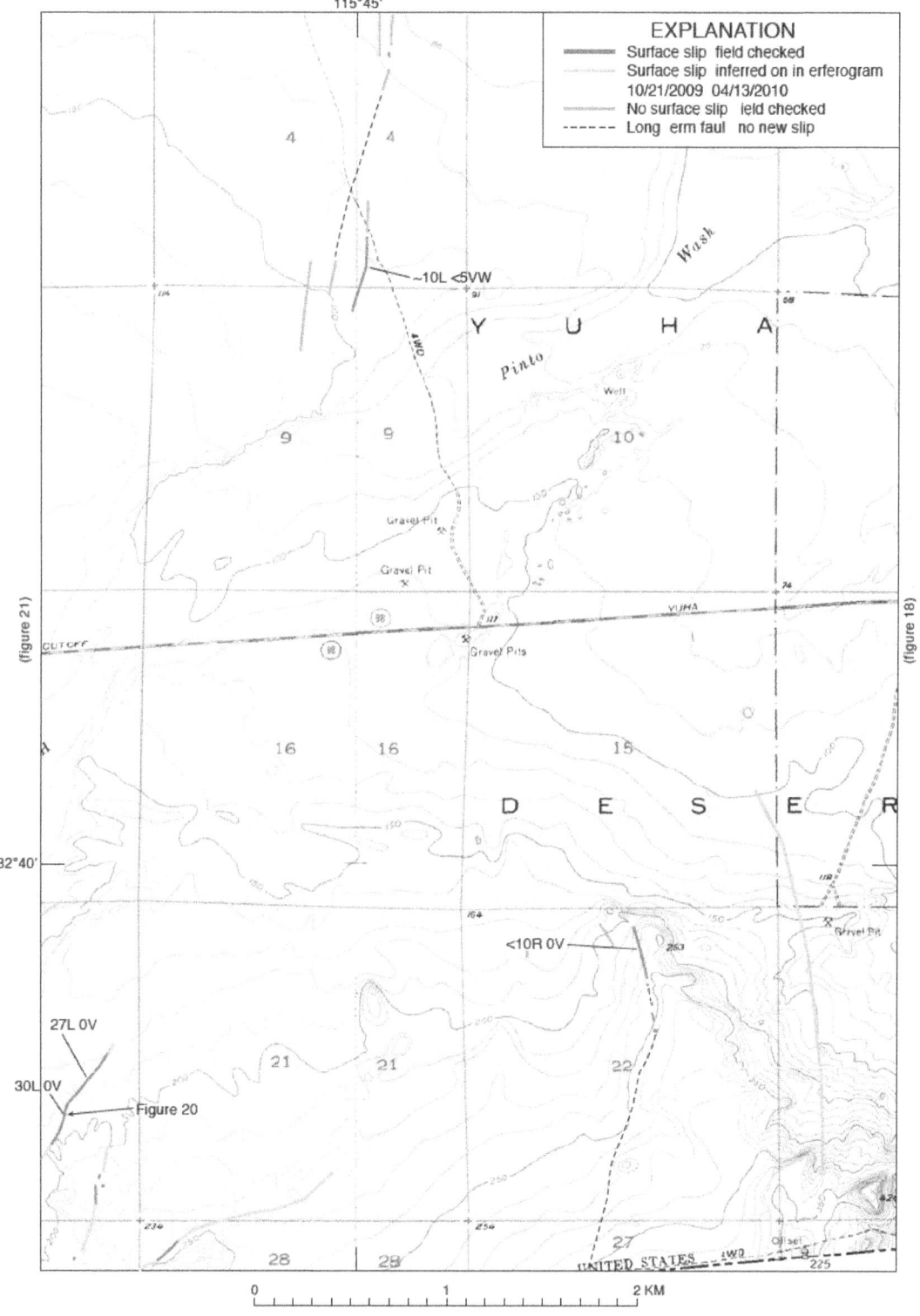

Figure 19. Map of faults and surface fractures in eastern Yuha Desert. Faults shown include elements of the Northern Centinela Fault Zone (Sections 14 and 15, 22 and 23), Yuha Fault (sections 4 and 9) and faults south of Pinto Wash (Section 20, 21, 28, and 29). Amount of slip shown in millimeters for both right-lateral (R), or left-lateral (L), and vertical (V) components. Vertical component of slip, where present, is indicated with either west (W) or east (E) side up. Map base from portions of the Mount Signal and Yuha Basin 7 1/2-minute topographic quadrangles. See figure 17 for location of map area.

Figure 20. Photograph of surface fractures along fault south of Pinto Wash; view to the northeast. See figure 19 for location. Photograph taken June 18, 2010, by J.A. Treiman.

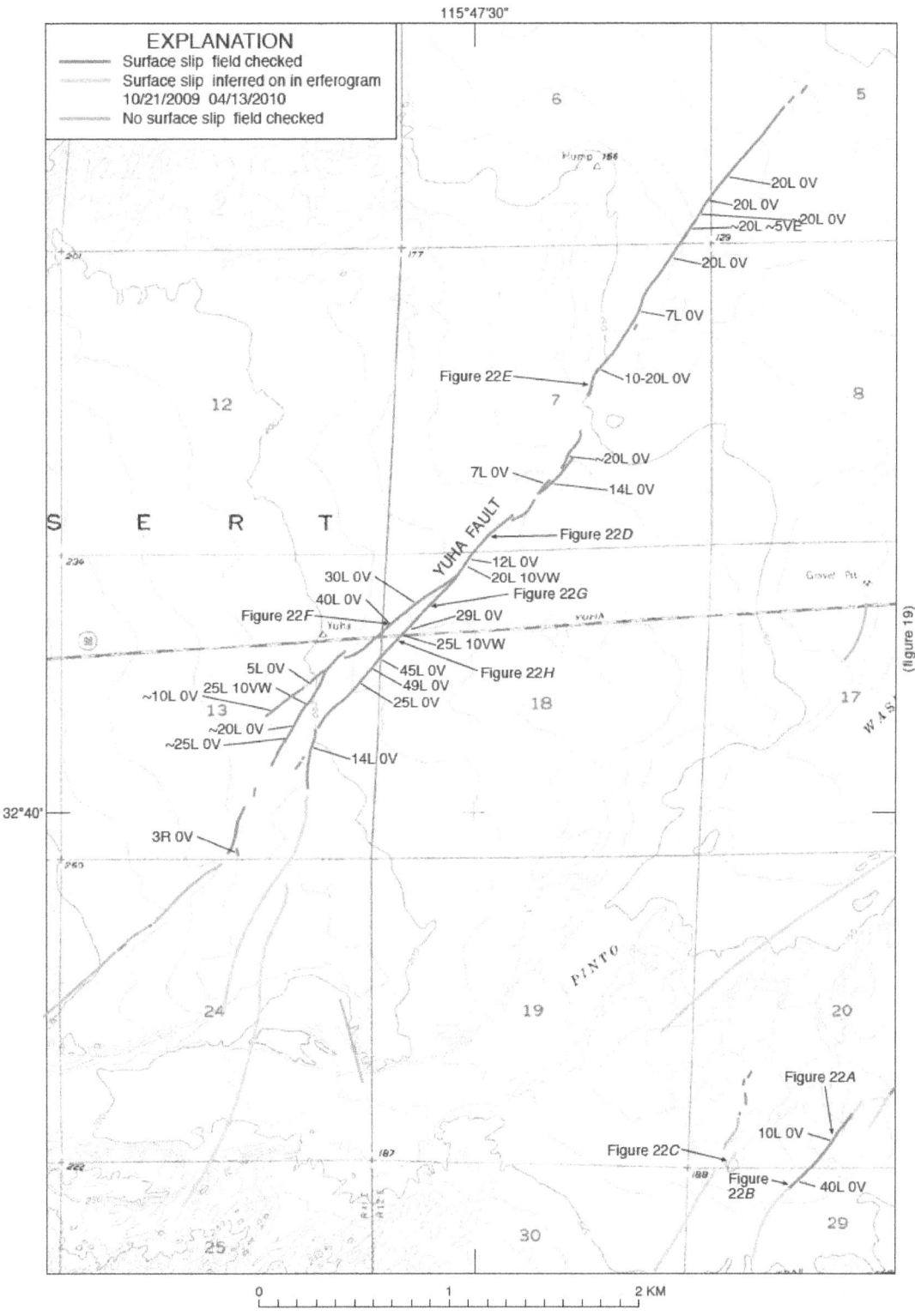

Figure 21. Map of faults and surface fractures in central Yuha Desert. Faults shown are the Yuha Fault and several faults south of Pinto Wash (Sections 20, 29–30). Amount of slip shown in millimeters for both right-lateral (R), or left-lateral (L), and vertical (V) components. Vertical component of slip, where present, is indicated with either west (W) or east (E) side up. Map base from a portion of the Yuha Basin 7 1/2-minute topographic quadrangle. See figure 17 for location of map area.

Figure 22. Photographs of fractures and Quaternary fault scarps along faults shown in figure 21. *A,* Left-lateral fractures along unnamed fault south of Pinto Wash, pen for scale. Photograph taken June 18, 2010. *B,* Continuous left-lateral fractures along unnamed fault south of Pinto Wash (surface slip extends between red scale in foreground and geologist in distance); view to the southwest. This section of fault consists of a cemented shear zone. Photograph taken June 18, 2010, by J.A. Treiman. *C,* Shattered and overturned surface crust. Shattered ground may be partly a topographic effect, given that the site is on a low ridge adjacent to a fault (as indicated by UAVSAR interferogram), which had no new surface fault breakage. There may also be some lateral spread of the ridge toward a wash

immediately to the southeast (note fractures marked with white arrows). Photograph taken June 19, 2010, by J.A. Treiman. *D,* Fault scarp (at change in slope) with fractures (white arrows) along Yuha Fault; view to the northeast. Photograph taken April 7, 2010, by J.A. Treiman. *E,* Fault scarp (above change in slope) with fractures (white arrows) along Yuha Fault; view to the northwest. Yellow notebook (in center) for scale. Photograph taken May 11, 2010, by J.A. Treiman. *F,* Left-lateral fractures along Yuha Fault. White arrows mark matches across en echelon fractures. Photograph taken May 27, 2010. *G,* Left-lateral fractures along Yuha Fault. White arrows mark matching features across en echelon fracture; pen (15 cm long) for scale. Photograph taken April 7, 2010. *H,* Continuous left-lateral surface fractures along Yuha Fault, immediately south of State Highway 98; view to the northeast. Photograph taken April 6, 2010, by J.A. Treiman.

measured cumulative left-lateral slip on the two main traces of the fault totaling about 60–70 mm (the largest slip measurement on a single fault break was 49 mm; figs. 21, 22*D*, *E*). The Yuha Fault moved in association with the El Mayor-Cucapah mainshock, but also had a second episode of slip, sometime in late May to early June (see discussion, below, on timing and location of slips in the Yuha Desert area). The Yuha Fault exhibits some structural complexity. Not only are there two significant subparallel fault traces (see near State Highway 98 in fig. 21), but the northeastern end of the fault is characterized by several small right steps across low, narrow pressure ridges. A broader right step transfers minor displacement to a more northerly trending fault trace that is marked by a prominent vegetation lineament in older imagery.

Laguna Salada Fault, East Branch

The Laguna Salada Fault, east branch, had been mapped before the El Mayor-Cucapah earthquake (Dibblee, 1954; Clark, 1982; Isaac, 1986; and Kahle, 1988). The fault is a northwest-trending, right-lateral splay off a long, prominent fault in Mexico (see for example, Isaac, 1986; Mueller and Rockwell, 1995). Field checks for surface breakage along the Laguna Salada Fault, east branch, began 2 days after the El Mayor-Cucapah earthquake. Three of us (M.J.R., J.A.T., and K.J.K.) checked the Laguna Salada Fault, east branch, in the areas both north and south of State Highway 98 (figs. 17, 23) on April 6–7, 2010. On April 8, field checks were made near the U.S.-Mexico border (by J.A.T. and J.L.H.) and also farther north of State Highway 98 (by K.J.K., R.R.S., and P.J.I.). Triggered slip in the border area was revisited by J.A.T. on May 12, 2010.

Discussion

Triggered slip in 2010 along the Laguna Salada Fault, east branch, in the Yuha Desert area occurred along previously mapped fault traces (fig. 23). We mapped nearly continuous fresh surface breakage for about 3 km on the south side of State Highway 98 along a prominent, preexisting fault scarp (figs. 24*A*–*C*). Farther south, the fault steps to the right, to a fault trace that we followed to the U.S.-Mexico border (figs. 23, 24*D*). A field check on May 12 found fresh displacement of a surface modified by recent (postearthquake) rainfall. North of State Highway 98, slip could be recognized by dislocations in UAVSAR interferograms along an additional 3.6 km of the fault, and field checking verified that along roughly 0.7 km. Measured slip amounts along the Laguna Salada Fault, east branch commonly ranged from about 5 to about 40 mm for the right-lateral component and 0–30 mm for the vertical component, up on the east side (fig 23).

Laguna Salada Fault, West Branch

Field checks for surface breakage along the west branch of the Laguna Salada Fault, another northwest-trending,

right-lateral fault in the southwestern Imperial Valley, began 2 days after the El Mayor-Cucapah earthquake. Three of us (M.J.R., J.A.T., and K.J.K.) checked the Laguna Salada Fault, west branch, in the Yuha Desert on April 6–7, 2010. Additional field checks were made along the fault on April 8 (by J.A.T., J.L.H., K.J.K., R.R.S., and P.J.I.), May 12 (J.A.T.), June 16 (M.J.R., J.A.T., and M.E.S.), and June 19, 2010 (J.A.T.). The Laguna Salada Fault, west branch, in California is about 6 km long. This fault extends southeastward of the border for several dozen additional kilometers (see, for example, Isaac, 1986; Mueller and Rockwell, 1995).

Discussion

Triggered slip in 2010 along the Laguna Salada Fault, west branch, predominantly occurred along previously mapped fault traces (figs. 23, 25); local structural complexities were revealed in the new surface slip, including at least two subparallel traces, both of which extend discontinuously to the border. The terrain between the two dominant traces is depressed, with preexisting scarps facing into the depression. We mapped nearly continuous fresh surface breakage for about 5 km. The fault is marked locally by prominent fault scarps (for example, figs. 26*B*–*C*). Measured slip along the Laguna Salada Fault, west branch, generally amounted to about 10–40 mm for the right-lateral component and 0–20 mm for the vertical component, up on the west side (fig. 25) of the western splay (fig. 25).

Yuha Well Fault Zone

The Yuha Well Fault Zone is a new name for what was previously called the Yuha Wells [sic] Fault, because there is only one well named "Yuha" and there is no single, throughgoing fault. Hence, herein we rename this set of northeast-trending, left-lateral faults the Yuha Well Fault Zone. The fault zone has a width of about 3–5 km, encompassing more than a half dozen individual left-lateral faults and, at its southwestern end, a series of normal faults (figs. 17, 25, 27). Two of the longer faults within the fault zone are the newly named Vista de Anza Fault (located near the southwestern end of the fault zone; figs. 17, 25) and the newly named (and restricted) Yuha Well Fault (located near the northeastern end of the fault zone; figs. 17, 27). The Yuha Well Fault Zone extends for about 10 km. The Vista de Anza Fault and Yuha Well Fault both have fresh surface breakage for about 4 km, and the latter fault appears to extend approximately an additional 1.8 km to the southwest, for a total length of about 6 km. Field checks for surface breakage along structures in the Yuha Well Fault Zone began 2 days after the El Mayor-Cucapah earthquake. Three of us (M.J.R., J.A.T., and K.J.K.) checked a short fault scarp in Section 12 (fig. 25) on April 6. The Yuha Well Fault was checked at Interstate Highway 8 on April 9 (J.A.T., J.L.H., P.J.I.), and no fractures were observed. Additional field checks of normal faults and the Vista de Anza Fault were made on

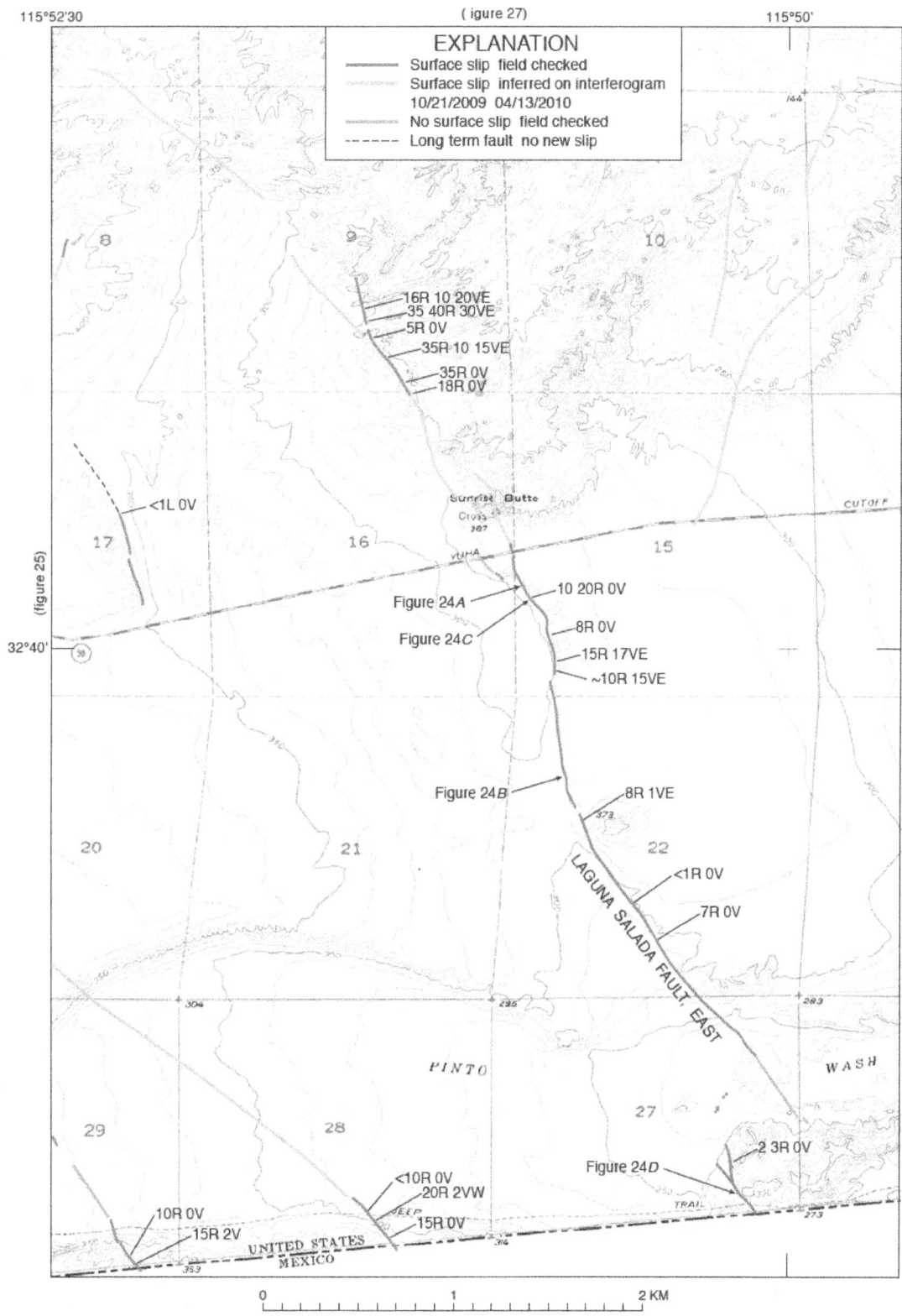

Figure 23. Map of faults and surface fractures in central Yuha Desert. Amount of slip shown in millimeters for both right-lateral (R), or left-lateral (L), and vertical (V) components. Vertical component of slip, where present, is indicated with either west (W) or east (E) side up. Map base from a portion of the Yuha Basin 7 1/2-minute topographic quadrangle. See figure 17 for location of map area.

Figure 24. Photographs of fractures and fault scarps along faults shown in figure 23. *A,* Fault scarp (at change in slope) with fractures (white arrows) along the east branch of the Laguna Salada Fault; view to the south. Photograph taken April 6, 2010, by J.A. Treiman. *B,* Fault scarp (at change in slope) with fractures (white arrows) along east branch of the Laguna Salada Fault; view to the south. Photograph taken April 6, 2010, by J. A. Treiman. *C,* Fault scarp (at change in slope) with fractures (white arrows) along east branch of the Laguna Salada Fault; view to the north. Photograph taken April 6, 2010, by J.A. Treiman. *D,* Fault scarp (at change in slope) with fractures (white arrows) along east branch of the Laguna Salada Fault; view to the south. Location of U.S.-Mexico border fence marked with yellow arrow. Photograph taken April 8, 2010, by J.A. Treiman.

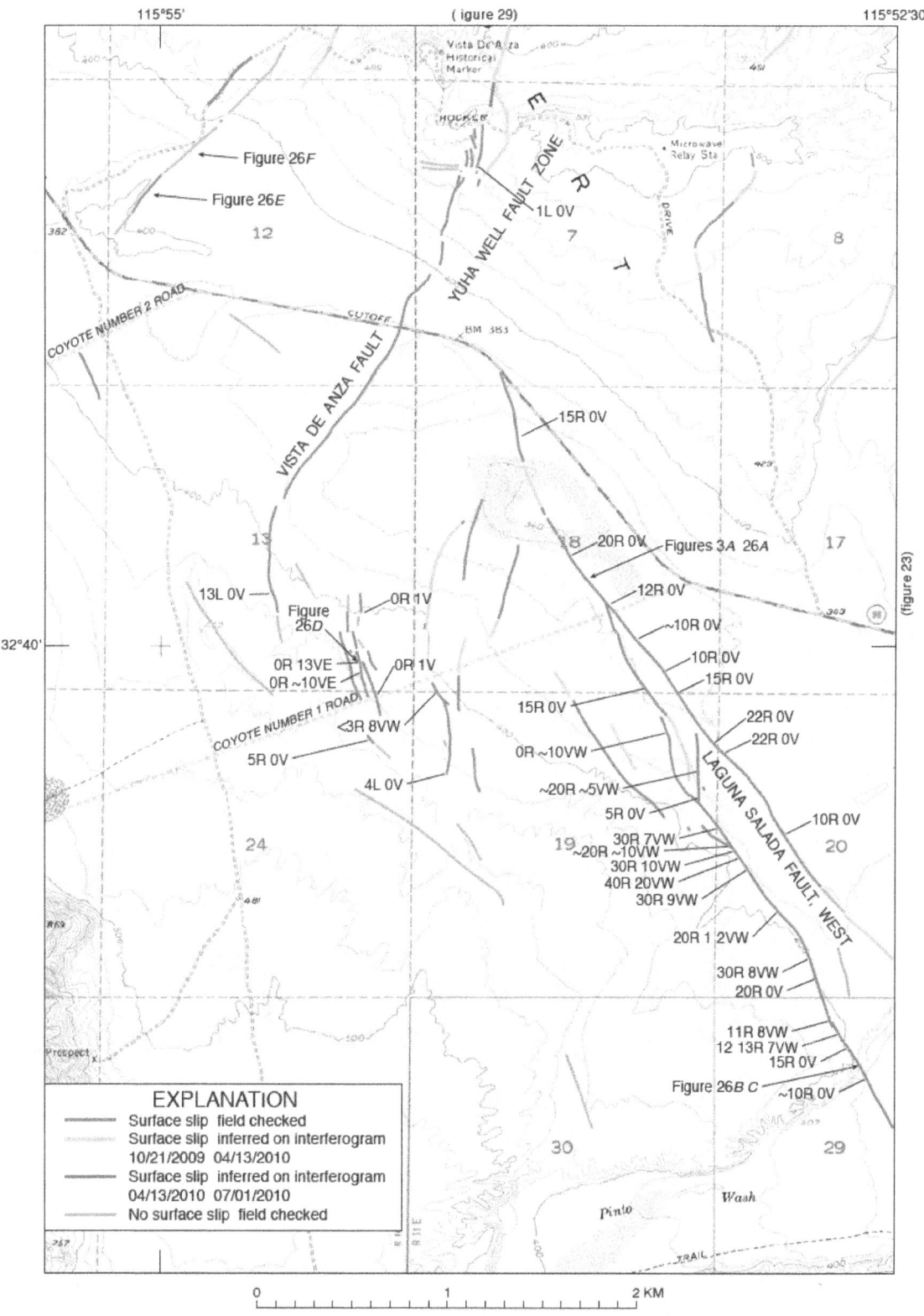

Figure 25. Map of faults and surface fractures in the central Yuha Desert. Faults include the west branch of the Laguna Salada Fault and the southwestern end of the Yuha Well Fault Zone. Amount of slip shown in millimeters for both right-lateral (R), or left-lateral (L), and vertical (V) components. Vertical component of slip, where present, is indicated with either west (W) or east (E) side up. Map base from a portion of the Coyote Wells 7 1/2-minute topographic quadrangle. See figure 17 for location of map area.

Figure 26. Photographs of fractures and fault scarps along faults shown in figure 25. *A,* Left-stepping, semicontinuous fractures with right-lateral offset and local "tent" structures along the Laguna Salada Fault, west branch; view to the northwest. Pen (circled) for scale. Photograph taken April 6, 2010. *B,* Fault scarp (white arrows) along Laguna Salada Fault, west branch. View to the west. Photo C is at leftmost arrow. Photograph taken April 7, 2010, by J.A. Treiman. *C,* Fault scarp (at change in slope, about 1 m in front of person) along Laguna Salada Fault, west branch; view to the south. Photograph taken April 7, 2010, by J.A. Treiman. *D,* Fault scarp (at change in slope) with fractures (black arrows) along one of several normal faults within an extensional zone near the juncture between the Laguna Salada Fault Zone and the Yuha Well Fault Zone; view to the north. Photograph taken May 12, 2010, by J.A. Treiman. *E,* Fault scarp (white arrows) along a northeast-trending fault within the Yuha Well Fault Zone; view to the northeast. Photograph taken April 6, 2010, by J.A. Treiman. *F,* Fault scarp (white arrows) along a fault within the Yuha Well Fault Zone; view to the southwest. Black arrow (and white outline), vehicle for scale. Photograph taken May 11, 2010, by J.A. Treiman.

May 11–12, 2010 (by J.A.T., and K.J.K.) and on June 16-19 (by J.A.T., M.J.R., and M.E.S.). The Yuha Well Fault and other parallel strands in Section 29 (fig. 27) were checked on June 18, 2010 (M.J.R. and J.A.T.). Triggered slip is inferred along several additional northeast-trending faults located between the Yuha Well Fault Zone and the Yuha Fault (figs. 17 and 27). This inference is based on relatively strong lineaments in interferograms derived from the UAVSAR data. These faults were not field checked.

Discussion

Triggered slip in 2010 along the Yuha Well Fault Zone occurred locally along a few previously mapped fault traces, but structural complexities and numerous additional faults were also revealed by the new surface slip. We mapped nearly continuous fresh surface breakage for about 3 km along the Vista de Anza Fault (fig. 25). Measured slip along structures within the Yuha Well Fault Zone commonly was small (largest left-lateral component was 19 mm); most slip was in the range of 1–3 mm, and piercing points were too poorly defined to allow precise measures. In spite of minimal amounts of slip in this event, discontinuous fault scarps (indicating preexistence of the faults) were common (figs. 26E, F). At its southwestern end, the fault zone bends southward into a series of subparallel normal faults, some with small components of right-lateral or left-lateral offset (figs. 25, 26D). All of the observed normal displacements are on preexisting scarps. However, some of the more prominent northwest-trending scarps showed no evidence of surface slip in the 2010 series of earthquakes (green lines in fig. 25).

June 14 M_w5.7 Aftershock

In our presentation of triggered slip in the Yuha Desert area (see detailed maps and photographs in figs. 17–29) all discussion has been relative to slip associated with the El Mayor-Cucapah mainshock of April 4, 2010. In our presentation that follows, all or nearly all of the triggered slip is associated with an M_w5.7 aftershock on June 14, 2010 (local, Pacific time; see fig 17) whose epicenter was near Ocotillo in the Yuha Desert. Up until June 14, 2010, most of the aftershock activity was confined to south of the Yuha Well Fault Zone.

On April 10, 2010, one of us (R.B.) installed creepmeters across both the east and west branches of the Laguna Salada Fault (figs. 17, 30). The creepmeter across the Laguna Salada Fault, west branch, recorded 2.2 mm of dextral slip at the time of the M_w5.7 aftershock on June 14, 2010 (local time; June 15, GMT). A continuous recorder was not installed on the east branch until August, but a caliper with 10-μm resolution showed no offset between May and August. Nor was slip observed on any other of the nearby creepmeters at the time of this large aftershock (fig. 30).

Slip rates were corrected for thermoelastic effects. The thermoelastic correction was undertaken by deriving a linear regression between the creepmeter signal and a 12-bit temperature recording and subtracting this empirically derived temperature correction from the creepmeter time-series. The correction effectively suppresses the direct effects of temperature on the graphite rod, but it does not correct for thermoelastic changes in the ground with phase lags other than 0°.

A plot of dextral slip versus time suggests that the Laguna Salada Fault, west branch, may be creeping steadily at 1–2 mm/yr, a rate that is similar to the Superstition Hills Fault in the same time period (June 15 to October 20, 2010). The slip rate on the east branch of the Laguna Salada Fault is also similar, but the record is too short to provide well-constrained rates. The slow background creep rate interrupted by abrupt slip events is almost certainly a manifestation of behavior similar to that described by Bilham and Behr (1992) on the Superstition Hills Fault. Slow continuous slip occurs in the near surface, whereas large episodic creep events occur on the deeper portion of the fault surface. Refer to Du and others (2003) for a discussion of the physical basis for this behavior in the presence of static and dynamic stress changes as applied to a creeping fault.

The aftershock on June 14, 2010, also triggered slip on faults to the northwest of those already discussed above. This slip is also visible in UAVSAR interferograms spanning the time of the aftershock occurrence. These additional faults are briefly discussed below (see also figs. 31–36).

Ocotillo Fault Zone

The Ocotillo Fault Zone is a new name for a group of northwest- to northeast-trending faults, some of which were previously recognized, but unnamed, before the El Mayor-Cucapah earthquake. The fault zone itself has a north-northeast trend and extends at least 6 km and maybe more (see fig. 17 for location). The Ocotillo Fault Zone includes many faults that did not display surface deformation in this earthquake sequence, as well as at least three that did. Most notable of the faults that did move is the Ocotillo Fault.

Ocotillo Fault

Field checks for surface breakage along a previously mapped (Smith, 1979; Clark, 1982; Kahle, 1988), but unnamed, fault in the southwestern Imperial Valley began 1 1/2 days after a local M_w5.7 aftershock of the El Mayor-Cucapah earthquake—the June 14, 2010, aftershock. Herein we name this fault the Ocotillo Fault, for the nearby community of Ocotillo. Two of us (J.A.T. and M.J.R.) checked the Ocotillo Fault in the area immediately east of Ocotillo (figs. 17, 33) on June 16, 2010. Field checks were made by walking along the whole of the mapped fault in areas of geologically young alluvial and fluvial deposits and, locally, loose sand. The Ocotillo Fault is about 1 km long and trends to the north-northwest (figs. 17, 33). Other fault strands, to

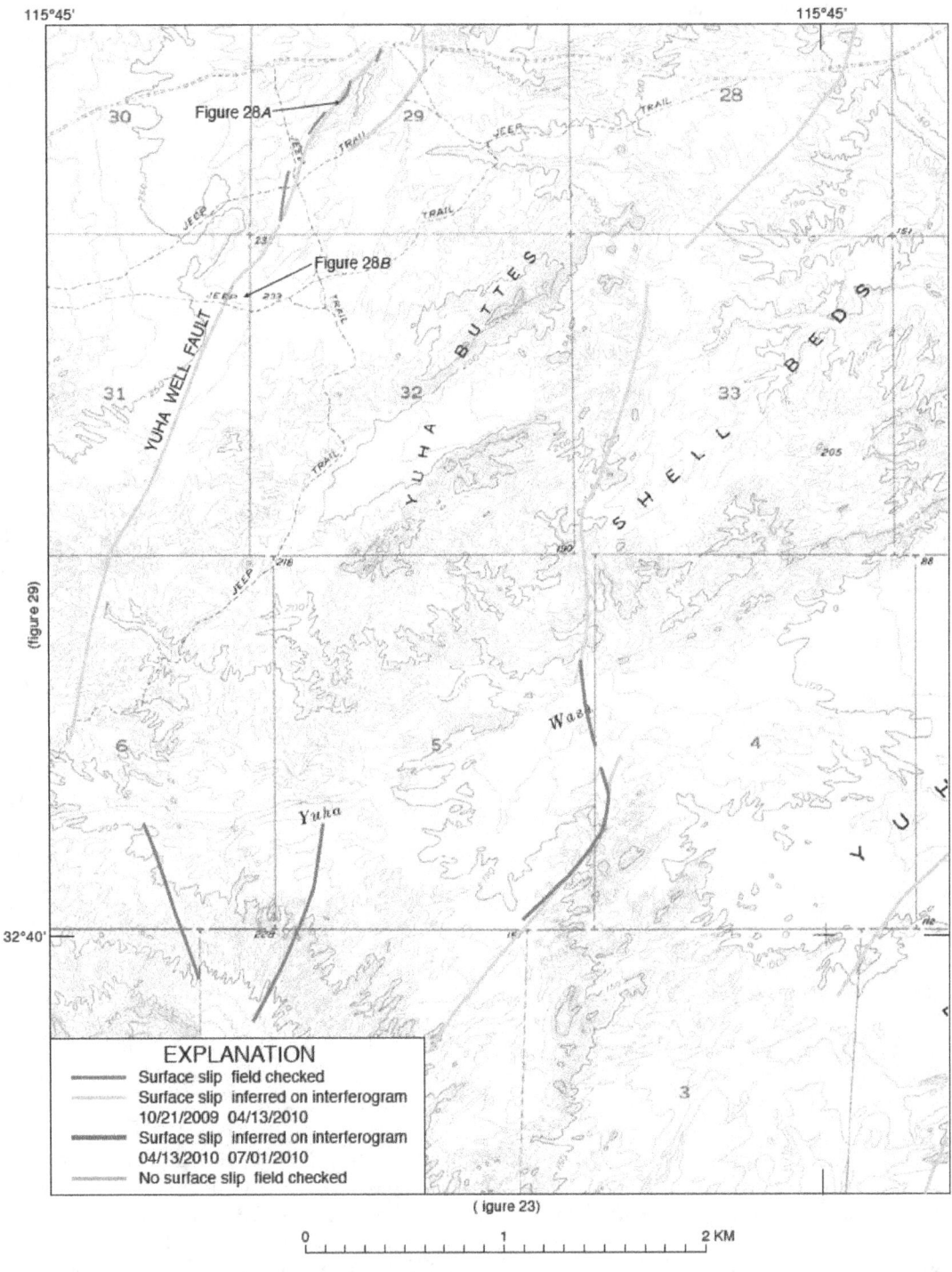

Figure 27. Map of faults and surface fractures in the central Yuha Desert. Faults shown are part of the Yuha Well Fault Zone. Map base from a portion of the Yuha Basin 7 1/2-minute topographic quadrangle. See figure 17 for location of map area.

Figure 28. Faulting and nonfaulting fractures along the Yuha Well Fault. *A,* Discontinuous fractures (black arrows) along a dissected scarp in the northeastern section of the Yuha Well Fault; view to the southwest. Person for scale (white arrow). Photo taken June 18, 2010, by J.A. Treiman. *B,* Pole aerial photograph of fractures unrelated to surface faulting; view to the southeast. This is an example of nonfaulting, earthquake-related features; here fracturing in concentric rings (white arrows) centered in recent alluvial fill. Youngest material at site appears to have been "tossed" by recent earthquake activity, possibly by the June 14, 2010, M_w5.7 aftershock (see text). Location of site shown in figure 27. Photo taken June 18, 2010.

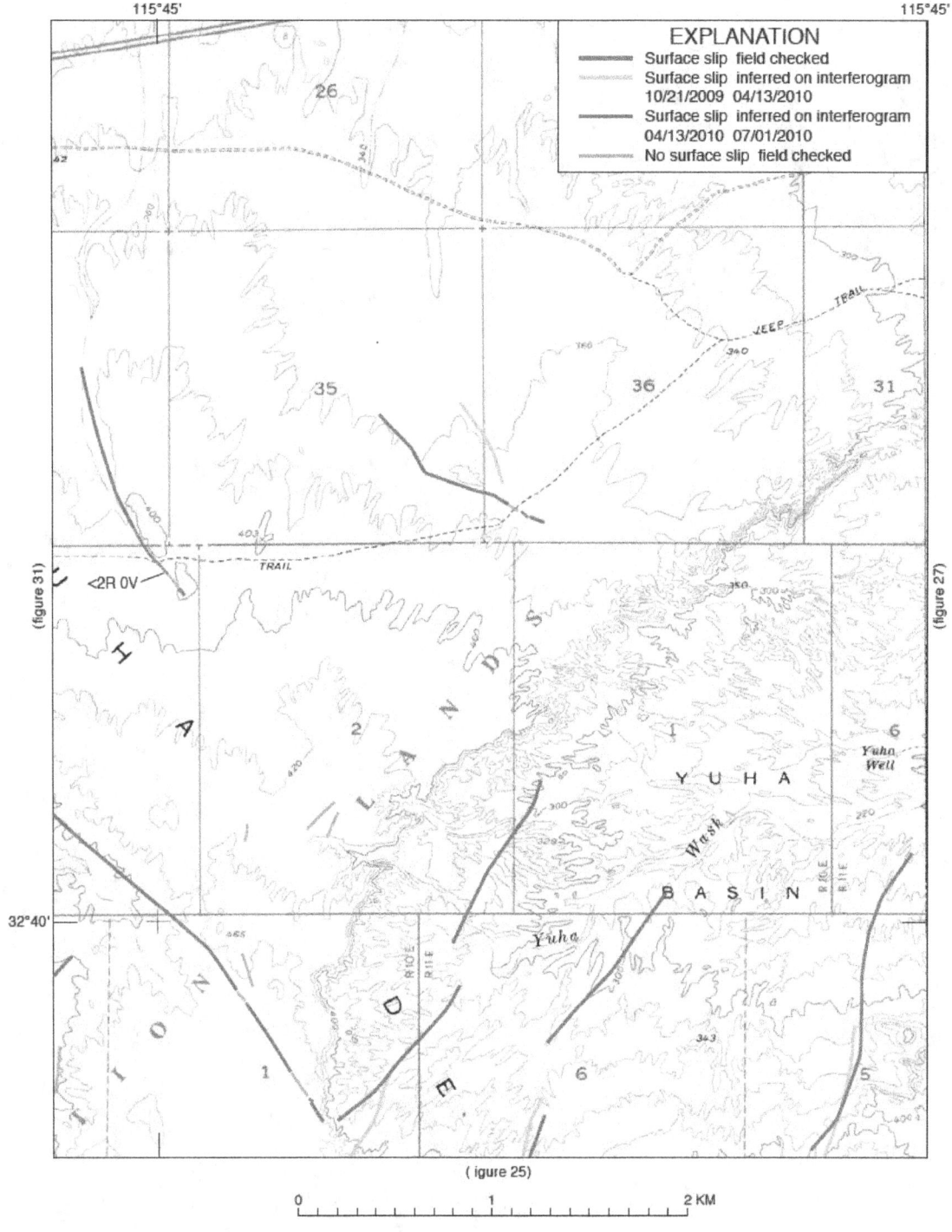

Figure 29. Map of faults and surface fractures in the Yuha Desert. Amount of slip shown in millimeters for both right-lateral (R) and vertical (V) components. Map base from a portion of the Coyote Wells 7 1/2-minute topographic quadrangle. See figure 17 for location of map area.

the north and to the south (figs. 33, 35), were also checked on August 2 (J.A.T.) and August 3, 2010 (J.A.T. and K.J.K.).

Discussion

Triggered slip in 2010 along the Ocotillo Fault in the southwestern Imperial Valley occurred along a preexisting scarp with a pronounced vegetation lineament. We mapped continuous, fresh surface breakage along the Ocotillo Fault for its whole 1-km length. The southern end of surface slip is about 110 m north of I-8 (fig. 33). Measured slip along the Ocotillo Fault was the largest measured in the entire earthquake sequence. Vertical components of slip of about 50–85 mm were measured, up on the east side (figs. 34A, C–F). Locally we observed left-stepping breaks, suggestive of a right-lateral component of slip (fig. 34B) and we did, in fact, measure 10–20 mm of right-lateral slip nearby (fig. 33). However, slip most commonly was manifest as pure vertical offset (figs. 34A, C–F). Local structural complexity in surface slip along the Ocotillo Fault resulted in a wide zone of surface breakage. We observed discontinuous fractures in a zone as much as 8 m wide.

Within the southern Ocotillo Fault Zone, continuous surface slip was mapped along a preexisting scarp (figs. 33, 34G). Relatively continuous surface breakage was also identified to the north (fig. 35) and died out south of a preexisting scarp (fig. 36). Less continuous surface slip was also observed on a similarly oriented fault north of the Elsinore Fault (fig. 35, Section 18).

Laguna Salada Fault, Northwest Extension

A weakly defined lineament in the UAVSAR interferogram that postdated the June 14 aftershock suggested the possibility of a northwest extension of the Laguna Salada Fault, west branch, that projects toward the southeastern end of the Elsinore Fault Zone. On August 3, 2010, two of us (J.A.T. and K.J.K.) checked several locations along this lineament, northeast of the South Fork of Coyote Wash (fig. 31).

Discussion

Field inspection of several localities along the lineament identified preexisting scarps, supporting the presence of a throughgoing fault. However, little evidence was found to indicate that brittle surface breakage had occurred. On the basis of the strength of the UAVSAR interferogram data, we infer that fault slip probably occurred at depth, resulting in right-lateral shear too diffuse to map at the surface.

Elsinore Fault Zone

Field checks for surface breakage along the Elsinore Fault Zone in the greater Yuha Desert area began the day after the El Mayor-Cucapah mainshock. One of us (J.A.T.) made spot checks along the southeastern Elsinore Fault Zone (figs. 1, 17) on April 5 and again on April 11 (with J.L.H.). Field

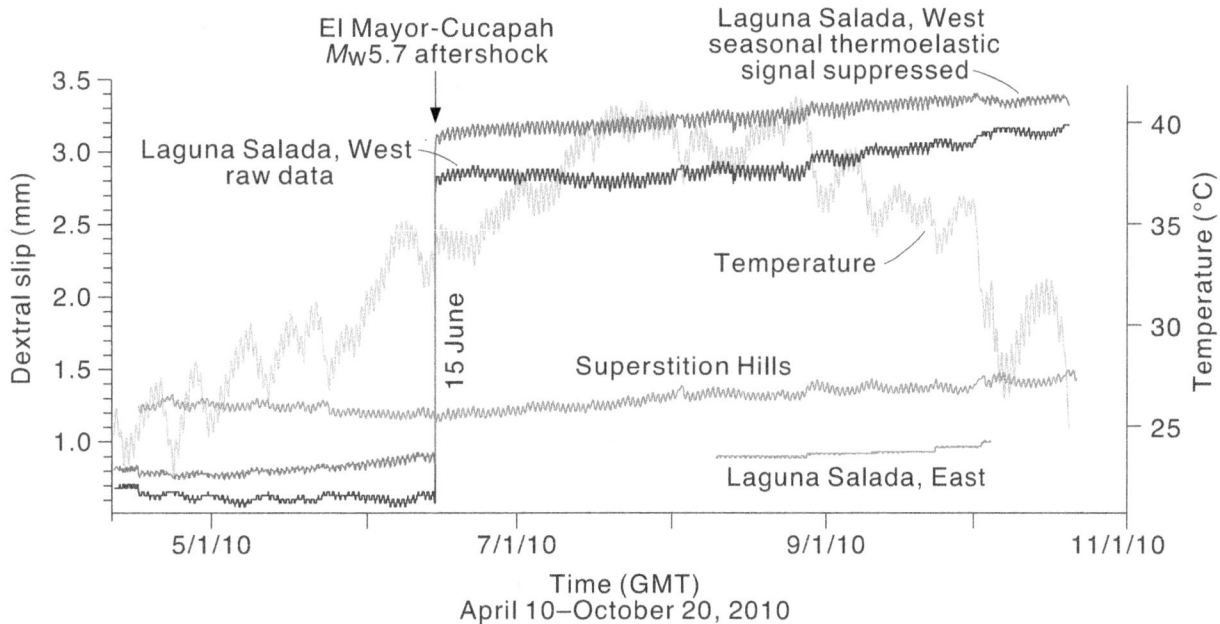

Figure 30. Creepmeter data for M_w5.7 aftershock of June 14, 2010, which was located about 7 km southeast of Ocotillo (fig. 17). Aftershock triggered more than 2 mm of dextral slip on the west branch of the Laguna Salada Fault.

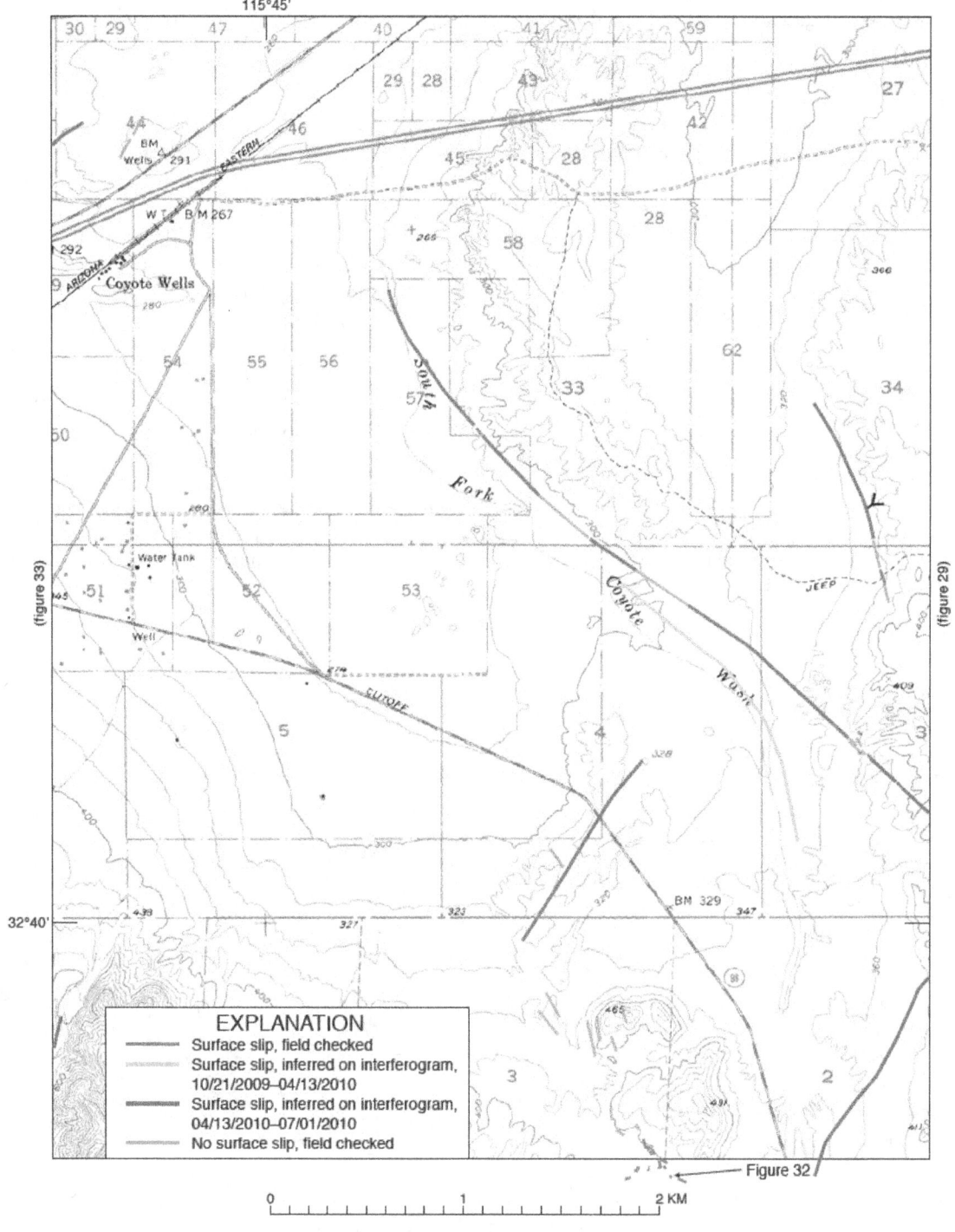

Figure 31. Map of faults and surface fractures in Yuha Desert. The principal structure is the inferred northwest extension of the Laguna Salada Fault. Map base from a portion of the Coyote Wells 7 1/2-minute topographic quadrangle. See figure 17 for location of map area.

checks were also made along projections of the Elsinore Fault Zone following the June 14, M_w5.7 aftershock. UAVSAR interferograms indicated new surface slip associated with that aftershock. Two of us (J.A.T. and K.J.K.) visited the area and mapped surface breakage on August 3, 2010.

Discussion

We saw no triggered slip along the Elsinore Fault Zone following the El Mayor-Cucapah mainshock; however, slip did develop along the southeastmost projection of the Elsinore Fault Zone in association with the June 14, 2010, M_w5.7 aftershock (figs. 17, 35). We mapped surface breakage in short sections (about 150 to 300 m long) in a zone of structural complexity (figs. 17, 35). The short breaks are in a stepover zone that forms a graben along the southward projection of the Elsinore Fault Zone where the Ocotillo Fault Zone would cross it. Slip was small; we measured as much as 10 mm right-lateral slip, without any appreciable vertical component of slip.

Other Faults

The 2010 El Mayor-Cucapah earthquake may have triggered surface slip on faults in the central Salton Trough or in the greater Yuha Desert area in addition to the ones we document in this report. Faults checked in the field that did not have surface slip include the Superstition Mountain Fault, several individual faults in the Elmore Ranch Fault Zone near State Highway 86 (although other faults closer to the

Figure 32. Photograph of fractures along an unnamed fault shown in figure 31. This isolated zone of minor fractures lies 2 kilometers southwest of the Laguna Salada Fault.

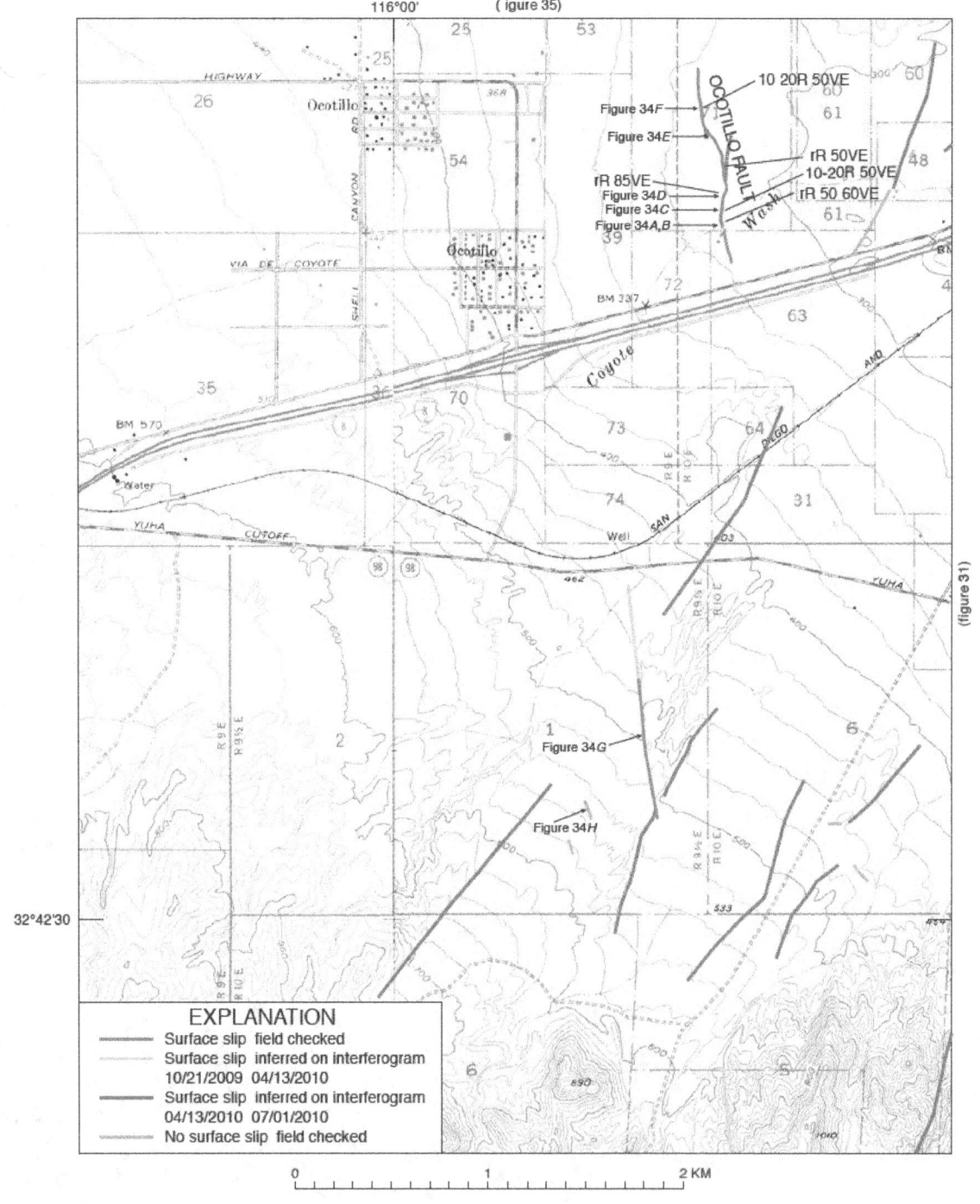

Figure 33. Map of faults and surface fractures in the Yuha Desert surrounding the community of Ocotillo. Amount of slip shown in millimeters for both right-lateral (R) and vertical (V) components. Vertical component of slip, where present, is indicated with either west (W) or east (E) side up. 'tr' indicates trace amount. Map base from portions of the Coyote Wells and In-Ko-Pa Gorge 7 1/2-minute topographic quadrangles. See figure 17 for location of map area.

Figure 34. Photographs of fractures and fault scarps along faults shown in figure 33. *A,* Vertical surface fractures along Ocotillo Fault. Faulting here is associated with the nearby M_w5.7 aftershock of June 14, 2010. Photograph taken June 16, 2010. *B,* Left-stepping, right-oblique surface fractures along Ocotillo Fault in loose sand. Photograph shows en echelon 'breaks' (black arrows) in loose sand, suggestive of slight right-lateral component of slip; red ruler for scale. Photograph taken June 16, 2010. *C,* Fractures along Ocotillo Fault at base of preexisting west-facing scarp. View to northeast. Photograph taken June 16, 2010, by J.A. Treiman. *D,* Fractures along Ocotillo Fault in recent wash deposits; view to the southeast. Photograph taken June 16, 2010, by J.A. Treiman. *E,* Right-oblique fractures along Ocotillo Fault. Photograph includes brittle fault movement (on right) and diffuse fault slip in loose sand (on left). Loose sand section in this view includes fresh track from a sidewinder rattlesnake (to the left of red scale). Photograph taken June 16, 2010. *F,* Fractures with vertical slip along Ocotillo Fault in sandy soil; view to the north. Subtle fault scarp on east (right) side of fault. Photograph shows local structural complexity in rupture (in foreground). Photograph taken June 16, 2010. *G,* Right-lateral fractures along unnamed fault south of I-8. Black notebook and red ruler for scale. Photograph taken August 2, 2010, by J.A. Treiman. *H,* Photograph of scarp, about 1.5–2 m high, without fresh surface fractures; view to the northwest. Photograph taken June 16, 2010.

Within the figure image, label: *en echelon 'breaks' in loose sand* (panel B); *scarp* (panel C).

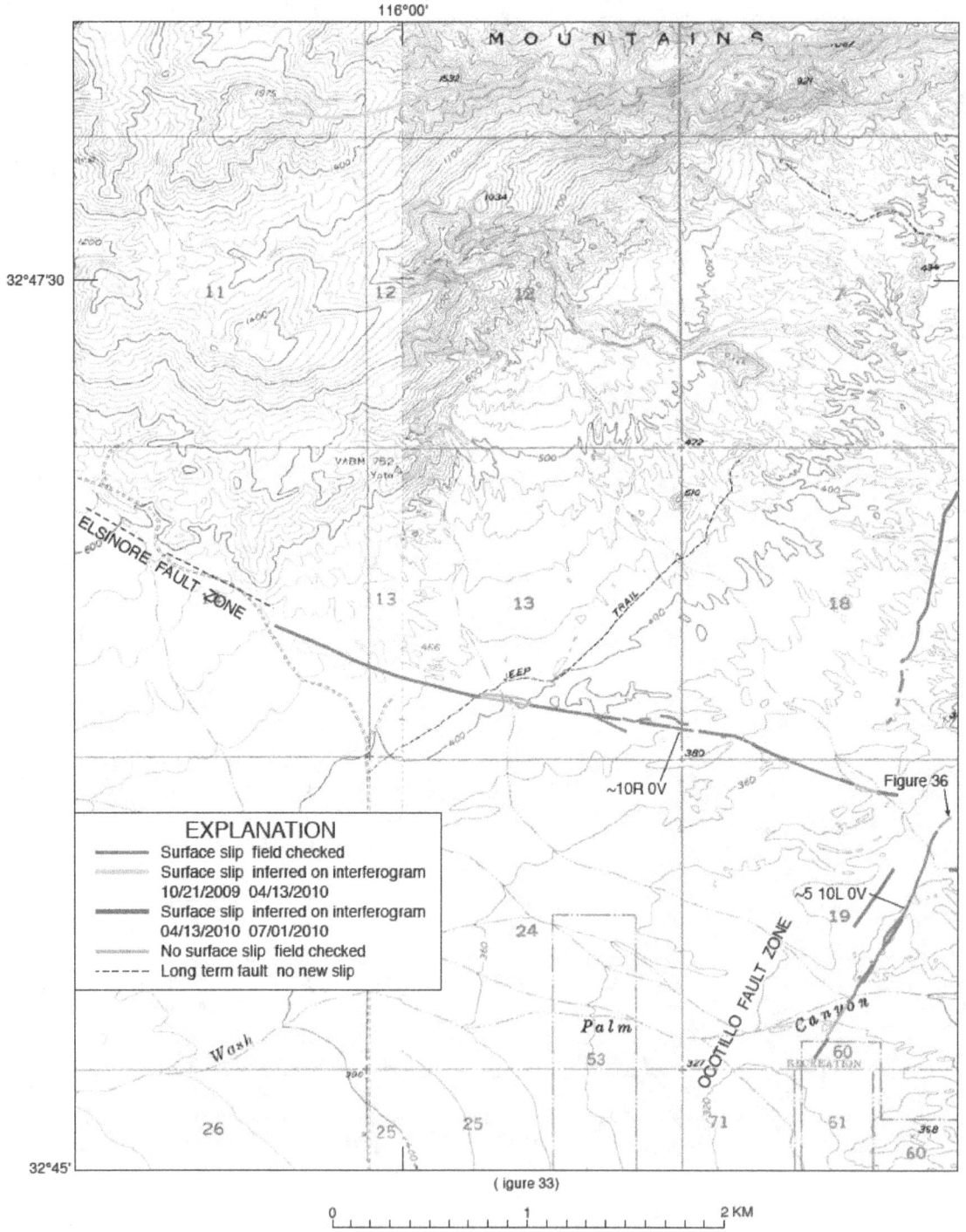

Figure 35. Map of faults and surface fractures in Yuha Desert. Amount of slip shown in millimeters for both right-lateral (R), or left-lateral (L), and vertical (V) components. Map base from portions of the Painted Gorge and Carrizo Mountain 7 1/2-minute topographic quadrangles. See figure 17 for location of map area.

Superstition Hills Fault appear to have surface slip features; see Wei and others, 2011), and the Rico Fault, near the community of Holtville. Field checks along numerous short faults, especially those west of the Laguna Salada Fault, west branch (figs. 17, 25), and those west of the Ocotillo Fault (figs. 33, 34*F*, 35), showed no evidence of surface slip.

Timing of Triggered Slip in the Yuha Desert Area

The location and timing of triggered slip in the Yuha Desert area are constrained by the new data presented in this report. Most of the red and orange faults shown in figure 17, especially those from the Northern Centinela Fault Zone to the Yuha Well Fault Zone, moved in response to the April 4, 2010, mainshock. This conclusion is supported by our detailed field observations and our interpretation of UAVSAR interferograms. A later episode of surface slip along the Yuha Fault is suggested by interferograms from ENVISAT (Environmental Satellite) flights in mid-May to early June. Surface slip may have also occurred on other faults, but the resolution of these interferograms is not as high as those of UAVSAR, and minor slip might have been overlooked. A third pulse of surface slip occurred in the Yuha Desert area in response to the June 14, 2010, M_w5.7 aftershock. This large aftershock triggered slip on faults farther to the northwest of faults that had moved in response to the mainshock (for example, along the Ocotillo and Elsinore Faults, figs. 33 and 35; see also purple lines in figs. 17, 25, 27, 29, 31, 33, and 35). The aftershock caused 2.2 mm of subsurface slip

Figure 36. Photograph of fault scarp along fault farther northeast of surface slip in 2010 (see fig. 35 for location). Small white arrow points to black notebook (with white outline) for scale. Photograph taken August 3, 2010, by J.A. Treiman.

on the Laguna Salada Fault, west branch, as measured by a creepmeter (fig. 30). Of interest, is the possibility of either afterslip or background creep seen in the creepmeter records shown in figure 30. A much longer period of measurement is needed to fully address these possibilities.

Acknowledgments

We thank J. Luke Blair, Roxanne Renedo, and Lesley Butcher (U.S. Geological Survey) for office assistance in this study. Ashley Strieg (University of Oregon) helped compile slip data from the Mecca Hills. Conversations with U.S. Geological Survey colleagues Ken Hudnut and Sinan Akciz, and Bill Bryant (California Geological Survey) aided the investigation and our conclusions. Kathy Haller, Pat McCrory, Sinan Akciz, and Tim McCrink provided helpful reviews of an earlier version of the manuscript. Grants that supported the creepmeter research of Roger Bilham include U.S. Geological Survey 07HQAG0026 and National Science Foundation EAR-1039474. Part of this research was carried out at the Jet Propulsion Laboratory, California Institute of Technology, under a contract with the National Aeronautics and Space Administration.

References Cited

Allen, C.R, Wyss, M., Brune, J.N., Grantz, A., and Wallace R.E., 1972, Displacement on the Imperial, Superstition Hills, and San Andreas Faults triggered by the Borrego Mountain earthquake, *in* The Borrego Mountain Earthquake: U.S. Geological Survey Professional Paper 787, p. 87–104.

Bilham, R., 1989, Surface slip subsequent to the 24 November 1987 Superstition Hills, California, earthquake monitored by digital creepmeters: Seismological Society of America Bulletin, v. 79, p. 424–450.

Bilham, R., and Behr, J., 1992, A two-layer model for aseismic slip on the Superstition Hills fault, California: Seismological Society of America Bulletin, v. 82, p. 1223–1235.

Bilham, R., and Williams, P., 1985, Sawtooth segmentation and deformation processes on the southern San Andreas fault, California: Geophysical Research Letters, v. 12, p. 557–560.

Blake, W.P., 1854, Ancient lake in the Colorado Desert: American Journal of Science (second series), v. 17, p. 435–438.

Blake, W.P., 1915, Sketch of the region at the head of the Gulf of California, *in* Cory, H.T., ed., The Imperial Valley and the Salton Sink: San Francisco, J.J. Newbegin, p. 1–35.

Bodin, P., Bilham, R., Behr J., Gomberg, J., and Hudnut, K.W., 1994, Slip triggered on southern California faults by the 1992 Joshua Tree, Landers, and Big Bear earthquakes: Seismological Society of America Bulletin, v. 84, p. 806–816.

Clark, M.M., 1972, Surface rupture along the Coyote Creek fault, *in* The Borrego Mountain earthquake of April 9, 1968: U.S. Geological Survey Professional Paper 787. p. 55–86.

Clark, M.M., 1982, Map showing recently active breaks along the Elsinore and associated faults, California, between Lake Henshaw and Mexico: U.S. Geological Survey Miscellaneous Geologic Investigations Map I-1329, two sheets.

Clark, M.M., 1984, Map showing recently active breaks along the San Andreas fault and associated faults between Salton Sea and Whitewater River-Mission Creek, California: U.S. Geological Survey Miscellaneous Geologic Investigations Map I-1483, scale 1:24,000.

Cohn, S.N., Allen, C.R., Gilman, R., and Gouty, N.R., 1982, Preearthquake and postearthquake creep on the Imperial fault and the Brawley fault zone, *in* The Imperial Valley, California, Earthquake of October 15, 1979: U.S. Geological Survey Professional Paper 1254, p. 161–167.

Dibblee, T.W., Jr., 1954, Geology of the Imperial Valley region, California, chap. II *in* Jahns, R.H., ed., Geology of southern California: Bulletin California Division of Mines and Geology, v. 170, p. 21–28.

Du, W., Sykes, L.R., Shaw, B.E., and Scholz, C.H., 2003, Triggered aseismic fault slip from nearby earthquakes; static or dynamic effect?: Journal of Geophysical Research, v. 108, 2131, doi:10.1029/2002JB002008.

Fletcher, J., Rockwell, T., Teran, O., Masana, E., Faneros, G., Hudnut, K., Gonzalez, J., Gonzalez, A., Spelz, R., Mueller, K., Chung, L.-H., Akciz, S., Galetzka, J., Stock, J., and Scharer, K., 2010, The surface ruptures associated with the El Mayor-Borrego earthquake sequence [abs.]: Geological Society of America, Cordilleran Section Meeting, p. LB1-4.

Fuis, G.S., 1982, Displacement on the Superstition Hills fault triggered by the earthquake, *in* The Imperial Valley, California, Earthquake of October 15, 1979: U.S. Geological Survey Professional Paper 1254, p. 145–154.

Goulty, N.R., Burford, R.O., Allen, C.R., Gilman, R., Johnson, C.E., and Keller, R.P., 1978, Large creep events on the Imperial fault, California: Seismological Society of America Bulletin, v. 68, p. 517–521.

Hauksson, E., Stock, J., Hutton, K., Yang, W., Vidal-Villegas, J.A., and Kanamori, H., 2011, The 2010 M_w 7.2 El Mayor-Cucapah earthquake sequence, Baja California, Mexico and southernmost California, USA; active seismotectonics along the Mexican Pacific margin: Pure and Applied Geophysics, v. 168, p. 1255–1279.

Hudnut, K.W., and Clark, M.M., 1989, New slip along parts of the 1968 Coyote Creek fault rupture, California: Seismological Society of America Bulletin, v. 79, p. 451–465.

Isaac, S., 1986, Geology and structure of the Yuha Desert between Ocotillo, California, and Laguna Salada, Baja California, Mexico: San Diego State University, M.S. thesis, 129 p.

Jennings, C.W., compiler, 1994, Fault activity map of California and adjacent areas: Department of Conservation, California Division of Mines and Geology, Geologic Data Map Series No. 6, scale 1:750,000.

Kahle, J.E., 1988, Preliminary map of the Quaternary faults in southeastern San Diego County and in southwestern Imperial County, California: Department of Conservation, California Division of Mines and Geology, Open-File Report 88-6.

Lohman, R.B., and McGuire, J.J., 2007, Earthquake swarms driven by aseismic creep in the Salton Trough, California: Journal of Geophysical Research, v. 112, B04405, doi 10.1029/2006JB004596.

Louie, J.N., Allen, C.R., Johnson, D.C., Haase, P.C., and Cohn, S.N., 1985, Fault slip in southern California: Seismological Society of America Bulletin, v. 75, p. 811–833.

Lyons, S.N., Bock, Y., and Sandwell, D.T., 2002, Creep along the Imperial Fault, southern California, from GPS measurements: Journal of Geophysical Research, v. 107, no. B10, 2249, doi:10.1029/2001JB000763.

McGill, S.F., Allen, C.R., Hudnut, K.W., Johnson, D.C., Miller, W.F., and Sieh, K.E., 1989, Slip on the Superstition Hills fault and on nearby faults associated with the 24 November 1987 Elmore Ranch and Superstition Hills earthquakes, southern California: Seismological Society of America Bulletin, v. 79, p. 362–375.

Meltzner, A.J., Rockwell, T.K., and Owen, L.A., 2006, Recent and long-term behavior of the Brawley fault zone, Imperial Valley, California; an escalation in slip rate?: Seismological Society of America Bulletin, v. 96, p. 2304–2328, doi:10.1785/0120050233.

Mueller, K.J., and Rockwell, T.K., 1995, Late quaternary activity of the Laguna Salada fault in northern Baja California: Geological Society of America Bulletin, v. 107, no. 1, p. 8–18.

Oskin, M.E., Arrowsmith, R., Hinojosa-Corona, A., Elliott, A.J., Teran, O.J., Fletcher, J.M., Saripalli, S., Banesh, D., 2011, Near-field coseismic deformation quantified from differential airborne LiDAR of the El Mayor-Cucapah earthquake surface rupture [abs.]: Eos (American Geophysical Union Transactions), Fall Meeting, San Francisco, T34C-01.

Rymer, M.J., 1989, Surface rupture in a fault stepover on the Superstition Hills fault, California, *in* Schwartz, D.P., and Sibson, R.H., eds., Fault segmentation and the controls of rupture initiation and termination: U.S. Geological Survey Open-File Report 89-315, p. 309–323.

Rymer, M.J., 2000, Triggered surface slips in the Coachella Valley area associated with the 1992 Joshua Tree and Landers, California, earthquakes: Seismological Society of America Bulletin, v. 90, p. 832–848.

Rymer, M.J., Boatwright, J., Seekins, L.C., Yule, J.D., and Liu, J., 2002, Triggered surface slips in the Salton Trough associated with the 1999 Hector Mine, California earthquake: Seismological Society of America Bulletin, v. 92, p. 1300–1317.

Rymer, M.J., Goldman, M.R., Catchings, R.D., Sickler, R.R., Criley, C.J., Kass, J.B., and Knepprath, N., 2009, High-resolution, shallow seismic imaging of the Brawley seismic zone near Obsidian Butte, Imperial County, California: Seismological Research Letters, v. 80, no. 2, p. 375–376.

Sharp, R.V., 1976, Surface faulting in Imperial Valley during the earthquake swarm of January–February, 1975: Seismological Society of America Bulletin, v. 66, p. 1145–1154.

Sharp, R.V., 1989, Pre-earthquake displacement and triggered displacement on the Imperial fault associated with the Superstition Hills earthquake of 24 November 1987: Seismological Society of America Bulletin, v. 79, p. 466–479.

Sharp, R.V., Lienkaemper, J.J., Bonilla, M.G., Burke, D.B., Cox, B.F., Herd, D.G., Miller, D.M., Morton, D.M., Ponti, D.J., Rymer, M.J., Tinsley, J.C., and Yount, J.C., 1982, Surface faulting in the central Imperial Valley, *in* The Imperial Valley, California, Earthquake of October 15, 1979: U.S. Geological Survey Professional Paper 1254, p. 119–144.

Sharp, R.V., Rymer, M.J., and Lienkaemper, J.J., 1986a, Surface displacements on the Imperial and Superstition Hills faults triggered by the Westmorland, California, earthquake of 26 April 1981: Seismological Society of America Bulletin, v. 76, p. 949–965.

Sharp, R.V., Rymer, M.J., and Morton, D.M., 1986b, Trace-fractures on the Banning fault created in association with the 1986 North Palm Springs earthquake: Seismological Society of America Bulletin, v. 76, p. 1838–1843.

Sharp, R.V., Budding, K.E., Boatwright, J., Ader, M.J., Bonilla, M.G., Clark, M.M., Fumal, T.E., Harms, K.K., Lienkaemper, J.J., Morton, D.M., O'Neill, B.J., Ostergren, C.L., Ponti, D.J., Rymer, M.J., Saxton, J.L., and Sims, J.D., 1989, Surface faulting along the Superstition Hills fault and nearby faults associated with the earthquakes of 24 November 1987: Seismological Society of America Bulletin, v. 79, p. 252–281.

Sieh, K.E., 1982, Slip along the San Andreas associated with the earthquake, *in* The Imperial Valley, California, Earthquake of October 15, 1979: U.S. Geological Survey Professional Paper 1254, p. 155–159.

Sieh, K.E., and Williams, P.L., 1990, Behavior of the southernmost San Andreas fault during the past 330 years: Journal of Geophysical Research, v. 95, p. 6629–6645.

Smith, D.P., 1979, Faults in the Yuha Desert: California Division of Mines and Geology, Fault Evaluation Report FER-91.

Stanley, G.M., 1963, Prehistoric lakes in Salton Sea Basin [abs.], *in* Abstracts for 1962: Geological Society of America Special Paper, v. 73, p. 249–250.

Stanley, G.M., 1966, Deformation of Pleistocene Lake Cahuilla shore line, Salton Sea Basin, California [abs.], *in* Abstracts for 1965: Geological Society of America Special Paper, v. 87, p. 165.

Thomas, R.G., 1963, The late Pleistocene 150-foot fresh water beachline of the Salton Sea area: Bulletin of the Southern California Academy of Sciences, v. 62, p. 9–17.

Van de Kamp, P.C., 1973, Holocene continental sedimentation in the Salton Basin, California; a reconnaissance: Geological Society of America Bulletin, v. 84, p. 827–848.

Waters, M.R., 1983, Late Holocene lacustrine stratigraphy and archaeology of ancient Lake Cahuilla, California: Quaternary Research, v. 19, p. 373–387.

Wei, M., Sandwell, D., and Fialko, Y., 2009, A silent M_w 4.7 slip event of October 2006 on the Superstition Hills fault, southern California: Journal of Geophysical Research, v. 114, B07402, doi:10.1029/2008JB006135.

Wei, M., Sandwell, D., Fialko, Y., and Bilham, R., 2011, Slip on faults in the Imperial Valley triggered by the 4 April 2010 M_w 7.2 El Mayor-Cucapah earthquake revealed by InSAR: Geophysical Research Letters, v. 38, L01308, doi:10.1029/2010GL045235.

Williams, P.L., and Sieh, K.E., 1987, Slow regular slip along the southernmost San Andreas fault for the past 40, 80, and 300 years [abs.]; Eos (American Geophysical Union Transactions), v. 68, p. 1506.

Williams, P.L., McGill, S.F., Sieh, K.E., Allen, C.R., and Louie, J.N., 1988, Triggered slip along the San Andreas fault after the 8 July 1986 North Palm Springs earthquake: Seismological Society of America Bulletin, v. 78, p. 1112–1122.

Appendix A

Appendix A: Table of slip data for the El Mayor-Cucapah earthquake, April 4, 2010.

Waypoint*	Latitude	Longitude	Date (mmddyy)	Fault Name	Sense of slip	slip (mm)	slip azimuth (deg)	slip plunge (deg)	fault strike azimuth (deg)	strike slip component (mm)	dip slip component (mm)
				San Andreas Fault							
KJK-391	33.65179561	-116.083555	042010	San Andreas	RL	2 - 4	307	0			
KJK-387	33.64980977	-116.0811158	042010	San Andreas	RL					7	
KJK-367	33.64450864	-116.0742608	042010	San Andreas	RL					5	
MW-SAF1	33.5726	-115.98153	050210	San Andreas	RL				334	5	
MW-SAF10	33.48531	-115.89091	050210	San Andreas	RL				324	5	
MW-SAF11	33.48461	-115.89023	050210	San Andreas	RL				334	5	
MW-SAF12	33.48289	-115.88838	050210	San Andreas	RL				324	6	
MW-SAF13	33.48181	-115.88746	050210	San Andreas	RL				334	15	
MW-SAF14	33.48077	-115.88627	050210	San Andreas	RL				324	5	
MW-SAF15	33.47993	-115.8853	050210	San Andreas	RL				324	9	
MW-SAF16	33.47721	-115.88155	050210	San Andreas	RL				324	8	
MW-SAF16	33.47679	-115.88085	050210	San Andreas	RL				314	3	
MW-SAF17	33.46632	-115.86591	050210	San Andreas	RL				324	6	
RJW-A	33.6067	-116.02432	041010	San Andreas	RL	1-3					
RJW-B	33.60732	-116.025067	041010	San Andreas	RL	3-5					
RJW-C	33.60830	-116.026500	041010	San Andreas	RL	8-12					
RJW-D	33.60927	-116.027500	041010	San Andreas	RL	12-15					
RJW-E	33.61092	-116.029650	041010	San Andreas	RL	12-15					
RJW-F	33.61325	-116.032617	041010	San Andreas	RL	16-18					
RJW-G	33.625267	-116.048267	041010	San Andreas	RL	5-8					
RJW-H	33.6258	-116.048950	041010	San Andreas	RL	7-10					
RJW-I	33.626433	-116.049617	041010	San Andreas	RL	6-9					
RJW-J	33.629134	-116.0518	041010	San Andreas	RL	2-4					
RJW-K	33.63015	-116.05258	041010	San Andreas	RL	3-7					
				Coyote Creek Fault							
JLH-513	33.1186496	-116.07681	041010	Coyote Creek	RL	7	303		340		
JAT-244	33.11640859	-116.074773	041010	Coyote Creek	RL					5	
JLH-502	33.11652851	-116.0750407	041010	Coyote Creek	RL				270	2	
JAT-242	33.11425209	-116.0727615	041010	Coyote Creek	RL	12	313		322		
JAT-240	33.11373174	-116.072268	041010	Coyote Creek	RL	11	311		325		
JLH-478	33.11372221	-116.0722624	041010	Coyote Creek	RL	11	313		322		
JAT-236	33.11214387	-116.0696501	041010	Coyote Creek	RL					2 - 3	

Appendix A: Table of slip data for the El Mayor-Cucapah earthquake, April 4, 2010—Continued

Waypoint*	Latitude	Longitude	Date (mmddyy)	Fault Name	Sense of slip	slip (mm)	slip azimuth (deg)	slip plunge (deg)	fault azimuth (deg)	strike slip component (mm)	dip slip component (mm)
				Coyote Creek Fault, continued							
JLH-451	33.11211681	-116.0696194	041010	Coyote Creek	RL					2 - 3	
JAT-235	33.11189175	-116.0691942	041010	Coyote Creek	RL					2 - 3	
JLH-449	33.118567	-116.0691937	041010	Coyote Creek	RL						
JLH-448	33.11079729	-116.0684208	041010	Coyote Creek	RL					2	
JAT-233	33.11025023	-116.0678048	041010	Coyote Creek	RL					5	
JLH-423	33.10768378	-116.0648999	041010	Coyote Creek	RL					15	
JAT-231	33.10684383	-116.0638244	041010	Coyote Creek	RL	12	304		332		
JAT-229	33.10559928	-116.0618825	041010	Coyote Creek	RL	16	318		333		
JAT-227	33.10427964	-116.0604448	041010	Coyote Creek	RL	16	314		335		
JAT-226	33.1040597	-116.060139	041010	Coyote Creek	RL					>10	
JLH-550	33.10403752	-116.0601175	041010	Coyote Creek	RL	15	316		323		
JAT-261	33.1037002	-116.0597152	041010	Coyote Creek	RL				326	15	
JAT-262	33.10324967	-116.0590179	041010	Coyote Creek	RL					10	15 dE
JAT-251	33.10292244	-116.0586477	041010	Coyote Creek	RL					10	
JLH-526	33.10255241	-116.0583235	041010	Coyote Creek	RL	10	294		335		
JAT-256	33.08383584	-116.0444535	041010	Coyote Creek	RL					>2	
				Superstition Hills, Wienert							
JJL-2	33.02216	-115.84962	040810	Superstition Hills	RL	6	284		299		
JJL-4	33.02061	-115.84336	040810	Superstition Hills	RL	5	305		282		
JJL-5	33.01938	-115.83814	040810	Superstition Hills	RL	5	283		299		
JJL-6	33.01773	-115.83292	040810	Superstition Hills	RL	7	294		296		
JJL-7	33.016	-115.82695	040810	Superstition Hills	RL	5	289		285		
JJL-8	33.01409	-115.82135	040810	Superstition Hills	RL	8	273		292		
JJL-9	33.01198	-115.81361	040810	Superstition Hills	RL	13	289		286		
JJL-10	33.00923	-115.8081	040810	Superstition Hills	RL	7	298		310		
JJL-11	33.00528	-115.80055	040810	Superstition Hills	RL	6	299		309		
MJR-A16	32.98455	-115.77065	040810	Superstition Hills	RL	11	272		293		0
JJL-13	32.99627	-115.78764	040810	Superstition Hills	RL	11	310		316		
MJR-A15	32.98126	-115.7658	040810	Superstition Hills	RL	5	273		285		
BPEO-SHF4	32.98042595	-115.7644845	040810	Superstition Hills	RL				300	10	0
BPEO-SHF3	32.97945499	-115.7629181	040810	Superstition Hills	RL		295		306		0 3 dE
MJR-A14	32.97842	-115.76128	040810	Superstition Hills	RL	10			294		
BPEO-SHF2	32.97726631	-115.7594258	040810	Superstition Hills	RL	12	274		304	8	0
MJR-A13	32.97651	-115.75828	040810	Superstition Hills	RL	4	285		300		0

Appendix A: Table of slip data for the El Mayor-Cucapah earthquake, April 4, 2010—Continued

Waypoint*	Latitude	Longitude	Date (mmdyy)	Fault Name	Sense of slip	slip (mm)	slip azimuth (deg)	slip plunge (deg)	fault azimuth (deg)	strike slip component (mm)	dip slip component (mm)
				Superstition Hills, Wienert Faults, continued							
MJR-A10	32.97597	-115.75759	040810	Superstition Hills	RL	6	290		296		1 - 2 dE
BPEO-SHF1	32.974509	-115.7553543	040810	Superstition Hills	RL	8	306		310		
BPEO-TOWER3	32.97275484	-115.7527471	040810	Superstition Hills	RL				303	7	1 dW
MJR-A2	32.97088	-115.75015	040810	Superstition Hills	RL	16	296		300		
BPEO-TWR3A	32.96771228	-115.7460094	040810	Superstition Hills	RL				307	9	2- 3 dSW
MJR-A4	32.96333	-115.74018	040810	Superstition Hills	RL	12	303				
BPEO-TWR3B	32.96324372	-115.7401139	040810	Superstition Hills	RL	11	310		324		1 dSW
MJR-A8	32.96024	-115.73742	040810	Superstition Hills	RL	6	283		303		0
BPEO-TWR3C	32.95924187	-115.7361711	040810	Superstition Hills	RL	11	308		318		2 - 3 dE
MJR-A6	32.9598	-115.73601	040810	Superstition Hills	RL	9	290		285		1 dW
JJL-34	32.95804	-115.7353	040810	Superstition Hills	RL	10	318		326		
JJL-35	32.95859	-115.73378	040810	Superstition Hills	RL	4	304		307		
JJL-36	32.95626	-115.73331	040810	Superstition Hills	RL	11	321		324		
JJL-38	32.95421	-115.73194	040810	Superstition Hills	RL	9	333		333		
JJL-41	32.95203	-115.72976	040810	Superstition Hills	RL	8	316		311		
JJL-39	32.95473	-115.72887	040810	Superstition Hills	RL	6	303		309		
JJL-40	32.95426	-115.72828	040810	Superstition Hills	RL	5	298		308		
JJL-42	32.95056	-115.72754	040810	Superstition Hills	RL	16	304		312		
JJL-43	32.94982	-115.72637	040810	Superstition Hills	RL	8	294		304		
JJL-44	32.94829	-115.72404	040810	Superstition Hills	RL	10	316		317		
JJL-45	32.94624	-115.72124	040810	Superstition Hills	RL	8	321		319		
JJL-46	32.94457	-115.71895	040810	Superstition Hills	RL	6	315		319		
JJL-47	32.943	-115.7169	040810	Superstition Hills	RL	15	307		314		
JJL-48	32.94137	-115.7149	040810	Superstition Hills	RL	9	304		317		
JJL-49	32.94022	-115.7135	040810	Superstition Hills	RL	11	296		317		
JJL-50	32.93887	-115.71179	040810	Superstition Hills	RL	15	316		315		
JJL-51	32.93747	-115.71003	040810	Superstition Hills	RL	14	321		322		
JJL-52	32.9365	-115.70878	040810	Superstition Hills	RL	11	307		315		
JJL-53	32.93513	-115.70711	040810	Superstition Hills	RL	16	309		313		
JJL-54	32.93369	-115.70532	040810	Superstition Hills	RL	16	303		317		
JJL-55	32.93247	-115.70381	040810	Superstition Hills	RL	15	319		317		
JJL-56	32.93154	-115.70259	040810	Superstition Hills	RL	16					
BPEO-CREEPM	32.93007016	-115.7007498	040810	Superstition Hills	RL	15	310		313		
JJL-57	32.93006	-115.70071	040810	Superstition Hills	RL	16	310		313		
MJR-A1	32.93007	-115.7007	040810	Superstition Hills	RL	16	310		313		3 dW
JJL-12	33.00095	-115.79378	040810	Superstition Hills	RL	15	308		309		

Appendix A: Table of slip data for the El Mayor-Cucapah earthquake, April 4, 2010—Continued

Waypoint*	Latitude	Longitude	Date (mmddyy)	Fault Name	Sense of slip	slip (mm)	slip azimuth (deg)	slip plunge (deg)	fault azimuth (deg)	strike slip component (mm)	dip slip compnent (mm)
				Superstition Hills, Wienert Faults, continued							
JJL-58	32.92601	-115.69604	040810	Superstition Hills	RL	9	319		318		
JJL-59	32.92219	-115.69114	040810	Superstition Hills	RL	13	321		314		
JJL-60	32.9191	-115.6868	040810	Superstition Hills	RL	16	306		314		
JJL-61	32.91604	-115.68226	040810	Superstition Hills	RL	10	300		317		
JJL-62	32.91328	-115.67751	040810	Superstition Hills	RL	13	314		317		
JJL-63	32.91045	-115.67407	040810	Superstition Hills	RL	13	297		322		
JJL-64	32.90688	-115.6706	040810	Superstition Hills	RL	10	304		309		
JJL-65	32.90303	-115.66532	040810	Superstition Hills	RL	15	319		322		
JJL-66	32.89883	-115.66076	040810	Superstition Hills	RL	14	319		316		
MJR-A17	32.8692	-115.64658	040810	Weinert	RL	5	290		348		0
				Kalin, Imperial, Brawley Faults							
MJR-Ao1	33.16214	-115.58318	041010	Kalin	V	3					
KJK-143	32.8832952	-115.5391058	040510	Imperial	RL	16	306	0		16	5 dW
MW-Imperial & Harris road	32.88366	-115.53905	050210	Imperial					014	10	
MW-Imperial & Harris road	32.88366	-115.53905	050210	Imperial					094	16	
KJK-143b	32.883222	-115.538306	040510	Imperial		12	294		004		19-20
MJR-796	32.88073	-115.53557	041110	Imperial	RL	7	295		315		0
BPEO-IF29	32.87855029	-115.5348338	041110	Imperial		12	294		315		
BPEO-IF28	32.8782177	-115.5344743	041110	Imperial	RL	12	338		333		
BPEO-IF25	32.87804067	-115.5343456	041110	Imperial	RL	12	311		329		10 dE
MJR-799	32.87721	-115.53354	041110	Imperial	RL	9	294		325		5 dE
MJR-Aa10	32.85461	-115.51724	040910	Imperial	RL	4	295		025		4 dE
MJR-Aa8	32.84707	-115.51148	040910	Imperial	RL	1	295		080		1 dE
MJR-Aa9	32.84707	-115.51148	040910	Imperial	RL	3	293		035		2 - 3 dE
MJR-Aa11	32.8398	-115.50931	040910	Imperial	RL	4	085		350		1 dE
BPEO-IF4	32.83981383	-115.5092884	040910	Imperial	RL						
MJR-Aa12	32.83315	-115.5012	040910	Imperial	RL					1	
BPEO-IF5	32.81947196	-115.4840488	040910	Imperial	RL					4	
MJR-Aa13	32.81945	-115.48403	040910	Imperial	RL	4	310		350		0
MJR-Aa16	32.78129	-115.44871	040910	Imperial	RL	4	313		315		0
MJR-Aa19	32.77386	-115.44413	040910	Imperial	RL	8.5	288		327		0
BPEO-IF15	32.76700795	-115.4389877	041010	Imperial	RL	5	311		330		0
MJR-Aa23	32.76692	-115.43897	041010	Imperial	RL	4	311		328		
MJR-Aa22	32.7593	-115.43189	041010	Imperial	RL					2-3	0

Appendix A: Table of slip data for the El Mayor-Cucapah earthquake, April 4, 2010—Continued

Waypoint*	Latitude	Longitude	Date (mmddyy)	Fault Name	Sense of slip	slip (mm)	slip azimuth (deg)	slip plunge (deg)	fault azimuth (deg)	strike slip compnent (mm)	dip slip compnent (mm)
				Kalin, Imperial, Brawley Faults, continued							
BPEO-IF13	32.7579689	-115.4307909	041010	Imperial	RL	4	300		325	~4	0
MJR-Aa21	32.75773	-115.43061	041010	Imperial	RL	7	325		355		0
MJR-Aa20	32.75186	-115.42575	041010	Imperial	RL	5	305		327		0
MJR-Aa25	32.73844	-115.41373	041010	Imperial	RL						
BPEO-IF16	32.7384156	-115.4137213	041010	Imperial	RL	7	283		333		0
MJR-Aa26	32.73025	-115.40605	041010	Imperial	RL						
BPEO-IF17	32.73015976	-115.4059965	041010	Imperial	RL						
MJR-Aa27	32.72613	-115.40242	041010	Imperial	RL	4	280		325		0
MJR-Aa7	32.86921	-115.52434	040910	Brawley	RL	9	315		080		2 dW
BPEO-BRF2	32.9036504	-115.4838825	040910	Brawley	RL	9	088		360		0
BPEO-BRF3	32.94469893	-115.4838342	040910	Brawley	RL	7	303		021		1 dNW
MJR-Aa1	32.90373	-115.48375	040910	Brawley	RL	10	289		011		0
MJR-Aa2	32.94495	-115.48372	040910	Brawley	RL	6	289		004		0
MJR-801	32.90956	-115.48074	041110	Brawley	RL	13	285		003		
MJR-Aa3	32.88295	-115.47996	040910	Brawley	RL					1 - 2	0
MJR-Aa5	32.8693	-115.47756	040910	Brawley	RL	11	283		017		
MJR-Aa6	32.84009	-115.47712	040910	Brawley	RL	10	273		018		
BPEO-BRF5	32.88295984	-115.4754282	040910	Brawley	RL						
MJR-Aa4	32.88294	-115.47538	040910	Brawley	RL	4	274		003		1 dW
				Yuha Desert Area							
				Northern Centinela Fault Zone							
JAT-395	32.66244471	-115.7347603	051210	Centinela	RL					<10	
JAT-703	32.65619516	-115.6975366	061910	Centinela zone	LL					10	
JAT-702	32.65593231	-115.6974346	061910	Centinela zone	LL	5	335		305		
JAT-695	32.66267538	-115.6839592	061910	Centinela zone	LL					~10	dE
				Faults South of Pinto Wash							
JAT-208	32.63947427	-115.8580507	040710	unnamed, NW-trending	RL					<10	
JAT-622	32.65335739	-115.7771767	061810	unnamed	RL,EXT					1 - 2	
MJR-225	32.64853586	-115.7739981	061810	unnamed, NE-trending	LL	20	087		054		
JAT-634	32.64936626	-115.7728959	061810	unnamed	LL					~40	

Appendix A: Table of slip data for the El Mayor-Cucapah earthquake, April 4, 2010—Continued

Waypoint*	Latitude	Longitude	Date (mmddyy)	Fault Name	Sense of slip	slip (mm)	slip azimuth (deg)	slip plunge (deg)	fault azimuth (deg)	strike slip compnent (mm)	dip slip compnent (mm)
				Faults South of Pinto Wash, continued							
MJR-209	32.65053931	-115.7718919	061810	unnamed, NE-trending	LL	10	054		042		
JAT-626	32.65195727	-115.7706804	061810	unnamed	EXT	5	115				
JAT-658	32.6366316	-115.768025	061810	unnamed	LL					30	
MJR-252	32.6560779	-115.766392	061810	unnamed, NE-trending	LL	27	064		043		
				Yuha Fault							
JAT-280	32.66511619	-115.8059246	041010	Yuha	RL	3	345				
JLH-602	32.66153193	-115.8108722	041110	Yuha							
JLH-606	32.66511512	-115.8059076	041110	Yuha							
JLH-613	32.66506648	-115.8058823	041110	Yuha	RL	3	345		335		
JLH-353	32.66914308	-115.804022	040910	Yuha							
JAT-215	32.6717788	-115.8038808	040910	Yuha	LL					~10	
JAT-408	32.67045379	-115.803076	051210	Yuha	LL					~20	
JAT-218	32.67104924	-115.8027382	040910	Yuha	LL	~20	012		353		
JAT-409	32.67122626	-115.8026309	051210	Yuha	LL					~25	
JLH-628	32.66936076	-115.8022956	041110	Yuha							
JAT-220	32.6720953	-115.8019603	040910	Yuha	LL	25	038		025		10 dE
JLH-310	32.67307293	-115.801886	040910	Yuha	LL				070	5	
JAT-287	32.67008364	-115.8017136	041010	Yuha	LL	14	016		03		
JAT-103	32.67309844	-115.7990367	040610	Yuha	LL	25	050		043		
KJK-244	32.67382071	-115.7983761	040610	Yuha	LL	39	220	0	214		0
KJK-242	32.67419656	-115.7979791	040610	Yuha	LL	49	225	0			0
JAT-100	32.67421961	-115.7979638	040610	Yuha	LL	40	223		037	45	
MJR-918	32.67586682	-115.7972763	052710	Yuha	LL				230		
JAT-97	32.67528713	-115.7968695	040610	Yuha	LL					10	
JAT-118	32.67545342	-115.7966388	040710	Yuha	LL	25	035		045	25	10 dE
MJR-727	32.67568	-115.7963	040710	Yuha	LL					29	
KJK-256	32.67564654	-115.7962676	040710	Yuha	LL	29	211	0	220		0
MJR-907	32.67681456	-115.7958357	052710	Yuha	LL	30	245		250		
JAT-124	32.67864525	-115.7931949	040710	Yuha	LL		027	0	043	20	10 dE
KJK-262	32.67892051	-115.7929826	040710	Yuha	LL	12	027		043		
MJR-733	32.67893	-115.79296	040710	Yuha	LL	12					
KJK-277	32.68260302	-115.7885784	040710	Yuha	LL	7	042	0	020		0
JAT-138	32.68262029	-115.78856	040710	Yuha	LL	7	042		020		

Appendix A: Table of slip data for the El Mayor-Cucapah earthquake, April 4, 2010—Continued

Waypoint*	Latitude	Longitude	Date (mmddyy)	Fault Name	Sense of slip	slip (mm)	slip azimuth (deg)	slip plunge (deg)	fault azimuth (deg)	strike slip compnent (mm)	dip slip compnent (mm)
				Yuha Fault, continued							
JAT-140	32.68245935	-115.7884795	040710	Yuha	LL	14			044	14	
MJR-746	32.68254	-115.78837	040710	Yuha	LL	14	045				
KJK-276	32.68252834	-115.788369	040710	Yuha	LL	14	044	0	045		2 dSE
KJK-284	32.6835117	-115.7876382	040710	Yuha	LL	26-30	020	0			0
JAT-144	32.68377364	-115.7874925	040710	Yuha	LL					~20	
JAT-328	32.68812954	-115.7856686	051110	Yuha	LL					10 - 20	
JAT-321	32.69105852	-115.783217	051110	Yuha	LL	7	042		15		
JAT-315	32.69373	-115.7812698	051110	Yuha	LL	20	030				
JAT-311	32.69521058	-115.7801271	051110	Yuha	LL					~20	
JAT-309	32.69596696	-115.7795585	051110	Yuha	LL				037	~20	
KJK-429	32.6966215	-115.7790299	051110	Yuha	LL	20	225	0	033		
KJK-435	32.69782196	-115.7778846	051110	Yuha	LL	20	217	0	218		
JAT-299	32.6954788	-115.7505155	051110	unnamed, NE-trending	LL					~10	
				Laguna Salada Fault, East Branch							
KJK-V	32.68325	-115.857639	040810	Laguna Salada, East	RL	16	325	0	350		10 - 20 dW
KJK-T	32.682861	-115.857528	040810	Laguna Salada, East	RL	35-40	340	0	343		30 dW
KJK-AC	32.68175	-115.857417	040810	Laguna Salada, East	RL	5	292	0	325		
KJK-I	32.680861	-115.856472	040810	Laguna Salada, East	RL	35	280	0	318		10 - 15 dW
KJK-365	32.67936291	-115.8560295	040810	Laguna Salada, East	RL	35	297	0	340		
KJK-357	32.67895916	-115.8557378	040810	Laguna Salada, East	RL	18			338		
KJK-B	32.679639	-115.855472	040810	Laguna Salada, East	RL						0
JAT-59	32.66925752	-115.8488668	040610	Laguna Salada, East	RL					10 - 20	5 dW
JAT-66	32.6674819	-115.8478261	040610	Laguna Salada, East	RL	8	330				
MJR-679	32.66621	-115.84749	040610	Laguna Salada, East	RL					15	17 dW

Appendix A: Table of slip data for the El Mayor-Cucapah earthquake, April 4, 2010—Continued

Waypoint*	Latitude	Longitude	Date (mmddyy)	Fault Name	Sense of slip	slip (mm)	slip azimuth (deg)	slip plunge (deg)	fault azimuth (deg)	strike slip compnent (mm)	dip slip compnent (mm)
				Laguna Salada Fault, East Branch, continued							
JAT-72	32.66577601	-115.8474881	040610	Laguna Salada, East	RL					~10	15 dW
JAT-91	32.65837312	-115.8459056	040610	Laguna Salada, East	RL					8	
MJR-704	32.65822	-115.84585	040610	Laguna Salada, East	RL					8	0
KJK-226	32.65820305	-115.845831	040610	Laguna Salada, East	RL	7	342	0	320 - 324		1
JAT-167	32.65439272	-115.8430357	040710	Laguna Salada, East	RL					<1	
MJR-767	32.65263	-115.84166	040710	Laguna Salada, East		7	147		155		0
				Unnamed faults west of Laguna Salada Fault, East; figure 23							
JAT-692	32.68781841	-115.8858545	061810	Yuha Well						~5	
JAT-52	32.67314136	-115.8720035	040610	unnamed, NS-trend-ing	LL					<1	
				Laguna Salada Fault, West Branch							
KJK-AI	32.677222	-115.896778	040810	Laguna Salada, West	RL	15	005	0	360		
KJK-162	32.67120254	-115.8946736	040610	Laguna Salada, West	RL	20	321	0	333		
JAT-536	32.66371608	-115.8941103	061710	Laguna Salada, West	RL					<10	
JAT-539	32.66327083	-115.8938313	061710	Laguna Salada, West	RL	18	148		154		
JAT-544	32.66169906	-115.8925653	061710	Laguna Salada, West	RL	29	147		150		
KJK-153	32.66882518	-115.8924627	040610	Laguna Salada, West	RL	12	172	0	161		
JAT-33	32.66714394	-115.8909024	040610	Laguna Salada, West	RL					~10	
JLH-183	32.6648401	-115.8902727	040810	Laguna Salada West	RL	15	320		327		
JLH-023	32.66557586	-115.8892856	040810	Laguna Salada West	RL	10	324		----		

Appendix A: Table of slip data for the El Mayor-Cucapah earthquake, April 4, 2010—Continued

Waypoint*	Latitude	Longitude	Date (mmddyy)	Fault Name	Sense of slip	slip (mm)	slip azimuth (deg)	slip plunge (deg)	fault azimuth (deg)	strike slip compnent (mm)	dip slip compnent (mm)
				Laguna Salada Fault, West Branch, continued							
JAT-185	32.66554534	-115.8892823	040810	Laguna Salada, West	RL	10	323				
JLH-173	32.6626308	-115.8891113	040810	Laguna Salada West	RL						~10
JAT-186	32.66455293	-115.8885152	040810	Laguna Salada, West	RL	15	323				
JLH-046	32.65950012	-115.8872327	040810	Laguna Salada West	RL	5					~5 dE
JAT-191	32.66080856	-115.8871902	040810	Laguna Salada, West	RL	~20	350-355		005		
JLH-033	32.66208994	-115.8863497	040810	Laguna Salada West	RL	22	315		320		
JLH-150	32.65801168	-115.8860575	040810	Laguna Salada West	RL	30	330		345		7
JLH-051	32.66164708	-115.8858587	040810	Laguna Salada West	RL	22					
JAT-192	32.6616025	-115.8858491	040810	Laguna Salada, West	RL					22	
JAT-198	32.65717149	-115.8854843	040810	Laguna Salada, West	RL					~20	~10 dE
JLH-142	32.65690005	-115.8852496	040810	Laguna Salada West	RL					30	10
JLH-140	32.65652371	-115.8849248	040810	Laguna Salada West	RL	40	328		340		20
JLH-138	32.65603089	-115.8845093	040810	Laguna Salada West	RL	30	310		322		9
JLH-129	32.65399122	-115.8827159	040810	Laguna Salada West	RL					20	
JLH-080	32.65762663	-115.8822306	040810	Laguna Salada West	RL	10			340		
JAT-195	32.65168905	-115.8808441	040810	Laguna Salada, West	RL	30	340				8 dE
JLH-119	32.65156758	-115.8807983	040810	Laguna Salada West	RL		340			30	8
JLH-115	32.65068984	-115.8804264	040810	Laguna Salada West	RL					20	

Appendix A: Table of slip data for the El Mayor-Cucapah earthquake, April 4, 2010—Continued

Waypoint*	Latitude	Longitude	Date (mmddyy)	Fault Name	Sense of slip	slip (mm)	slip azimuth (deg)	slip plunge (deg)	fault azimuth (deg)	strike slip compnent (mm)	dip slip compnent (mm)
				Laguna Salada Fault, West Branch, continued							
JLH-102	32.6486541	-115.8796667	040810	Laguna Salada West	RL	11	322				8
JAT-193	32.64777839	-115.8792026	040810	Laguna Salada, West	RL				340	12	8 dE
JAT-176	32.64740825	-115.87865	040710	Laguna Salada, West	RL	15	320		325		
JAT-173	32.64593303	-115.8776093	040710	Laguna Salada, West	RL					~10	
JLH-211	32.63732159	-115.8714138	040810	Laguna Salada, West	RL					10	
JLH-214	32.63696456	-115.8710247	040810	Laguna Salada West	RL	15	330			<10	2
JAT-208	32.63947427	-115.8580507	040810	Laguna Salada West	RL						
JLH-225	32.63898253	-115.8576089	040810	Laguna Salada West	RL	20	325		325		
JLH-235	32.63812363	-115.8567736	040810	Laguna Salada West	RL				325	15	
KJK-331	32.65258801	-115.8416863	040710	Laguna Salada, West	RL	7	147	0	155		0
				Unnamed faults; NW extension of Laguna Salada Fault, West; figure 25							
JAT-436	32.66610861	-115.906427	051210	unnamed	EXT	8					
JAT-362	32.66844213	-115.9063626	051110	unnamed	EXT	<1					
JAT-430	32.664773	-115.906127	051210	unnamed	V						
JAT-342	32.6624608	-115.9058798	051110	unnamed, NW-trending	RL	5	290		330		10 dW
JAT-831	32.72452712	-115.917011	080410	unnamed fault; figure 29	RL	<2					
JAT-420	32.66458511	-115.905558	051210	unnamed	EXT	<2					
				Yuha Well Fault Zone							
JAT-344	32.66942382	-115.9113033	051110	Vista de Anza	LL	13	355		317		
JAT-562	32.6816386	-115.9043349	061710	Vista de Anza	LL					<5	
JAT-497	32.6644671	-115.9018565	061710	Yuha Well	RL		072		020	~3	8 dE

Appendix A: Table of slip data for the El Mayor-Cucapah earthquake, April 4, 2010—Continued

Waypoint*	Latitude	Longitude	Date (mmddyy)	Fault Name	Sense of slip	slip (mm)	slip azimuth (deg)	slip plunge (deg)	fault azimuth (deg)	strike slip compnent (mm)	dip slip compnent (mm)
				Yuha Well Fault Zone, continued							
JAT-509	32.66082466	-115.9014649	061710	Yuha Well	LL		054		012	4	
JAT-518	32.66438663	-115.9009124	061710	Yuha Well	EXT, LL					~2 EXT; minor LL	
JAT-531	32.67266929	-115.9000702	061710	Yuha Well	LL					19	
JAT-731	32.67158568	-115.8975328	061910	Yuha Well	LL					10	slight dE
MJR-307	32.6832496	-115.8868301	061810	Yuha Well	LL	15	172				
MJR-298	32.68192543	-115.8865246	061810	Yuha Well	LL	12	175				
JAT-692	32.6878184	-115.8858545	061810	Yuha Well						~5	
				Ocotillo Fault Zone							
JAT-457	32.74616182	-115.9842379	061610	Ocotillo	RL					~10-20	~50 dW
JAT-451	32.74119973	-115.983047	061610	Ocotillo							~55 dW
JAT-452	32.7422297	-115.9830202	061610	Ocotillo							85 dW on main break
JAT-777	32.76239991	-115.9732086	080310	Ocotillo	LL	~5-10					
				Elsinore Fault Zone							
JAT-814	32.77069867	-115.9854985	080310	Elsinore	RL	~10					

* The waypoint designation is a combination of the initials of the observer (JLH, Janis Hernandez; KJK, Katherine Kendrick; JJL, James Lienkaemper; BPEO, Brian Olson; MJR, Michael Rymer; JAT, Jerry Treiman; MW, Meng Wei; RJW, Ray Weldon) and the notation made in their field notes.

www.ingramcontent.com/pod-product-compliance
Lightning Source LLC
Chambersburg PA
CBHW080436290526
45791CB00008BA/2522